MW00626332

THE COURAGE TO BE WEAK

THE PLACE OF BROKENNESS
IN THE MASCULINE JOURNEY

JOE STORR

Copyright © 2020 Howard J. Storr Jr.

All rights reserved. No part of this book may be reproduced or used in any manner without the prior written permission of the copyright owner, except for the use of brief quotations in a book review.

To request permissions, contact the author at Joe@JoeStorr.com.

ISBN: 978-0-578-51134-4

Library of Congress Number: 2019907382

First paperback edition June 2020.

Edited by Drew Tilton and Jessica Snell
Designed by Natalie Lauren Design Co.
Photography by Sanderstock

Unless noted, scripture quotations are from the ESV® Bible (The Holy Bible, English Standard Version®), Copyright © 2001 by Crossway Bibles, a publishing ministry of Good News Publishers. Used by permission. All rights reserved.

Scripture quotations taken from The Holy Bible, New International Version® NIV® Copyright © 1973 1978 1984 2011 by Biblica, Inc.™ Used by permission. All rights reserved worldwide.

H. J. Storr
JoeStorr.com

PRAISE FOR
THE COURAGE TO BE WEAK

The Courage to Be Weak took me on a journey that led me to surrender once again to the Lord Jesus and to trust Him with the deepest parts of my heart. Along the way, I did some deep spiritual work and the experience has been an important mile marker on my personal walk with Christ. With gratitude to Joe for his willingness to share his own journey of faith, I wholeheartedly recommend this book to all men who desire to walk in power and freedom with Jesus. May we all become the unique, authentic men of God that the Lord envisioned when He crafted us.

STEVE MAZZA, CHIEF OPERATIONS OFFICER
GSE CONSTRUCTION COMPANY, INC.

The Courage to Be Weak is for every guy grappling with what it means to be a well-developed man. As Joe reveals through sharing from his own journey, the road to becoming more fully ourselves, the men God desires us to be, leads us into our "broken places, our weak places." But we must have the courage to go there, and meet Jesus there. This movement into our brokenness with Jesus will be a huge paradigm shift for many men who desire to grow, and it is full of immense wisdom. The first thing I did when I finished this book was give it to my son. Be brave...read on!

MARK HANCOCK, FORMER DEPLOYMENT CELL COMMANDER
U.S. SPECIAL OPERATIONS COMMAND

It's said that you can only lead others where you have gone yourself. You want a guide who has been where you want to go and has the skills to lead you there. Joe is just that man who can lead men on that spiritual journey of brokenness and humility before the Lord which will lead to a deeper relationship with Him and the greater freedom and growth in Christ's image that our masculine souls long for. Come and let Joe be a companion and guide on a deeper journey with the Lord that could very well change your life.

BRYAN JOHNSON, SENIOR PASTOR
REVIVE COVENANT CHURCH

I would encourage every man to read this book! More than just a skilled communicator, Joe is an excellent relater. He invites us into his story, a quest for adventure and meaning. By most measures he is a "man's man"—a pilot, thrill seeker, officer, former U.S. Air Force attaché to Kazakhstan, strategically positioned when war broke out in Afghanistan shortly after 9/11. Yet, Joe's journey reveals the questions and struggles that so many of us face as men but are often unable to articulate. What was I created for? Why am I unfulfilled? What is my purpose?

The Courage to Be Weak is not a formula but rather a revealing of the character and amazing transformational power of God. It is a testimony of what can happen when we say yes to God, allowing Him access and permission to the hidden places of our hearts. It is an invitation into a place of intimacy with Jesus to find the beauty of brokenness (Psalm 51:16-17) and the joy of true humility— being willing to be known for who we are as well as who we are not. It presents keys to unlock the deep places that men rarely talk about to discover so much more—intimacy, healing, peace, confidence, purpose, calling, identity, and freedom!

I would also add that I believe that this book will bless every mother, daughter, sister, and wife. I recently heard it said that if you can heal the man, you will heal the family and heal the nation. Amen!

Thank you, Joe, for *the courage to be weak.*

LOREN JOHNSON, WORSHIP LEADER AND CHIEF EXECUTIVE OFFICER
CHRISTOPHER ENTERTAINMENT ORGANIZATION

Men, *The Courage to Be Weak* offers sound and practical application for growth in Christ to an area infrequently addressed by our ministries and friendships: our weaknesses. This book seeks to apply humility before God, real honesty with Him, and radical trust in God alone to answer the practical question: how can God use the "defeats" of my life to win the war of Christ-like growth in my life? Through the engaging story of his own life, Joe Storr explores topics related to our real weaknesses, and then asks relevant questions that help us to move forward in our walks with Jesus. I heartily endorse this book—I am recommending it to a group of men I meet with!

DOUG GERINGER, ASSOCIATE DEAN
TALBOT SCHOOL OF THEOLOGY

With verve, humor, and action, Storr uses his own story and military career to chart a life-giving path for men—and impart forward momentum—as they grow in their relationship with Jesus and in their masculine design. Great content...I really enjoyed this book!

JASON MCMARTIN, PHD, ASSOCIATE PROFESSOR OF THEOLOGY
TALBOT SCHOOL OF THEOLOGY/ROSEMEAD SCHOOL OF PSYCHOLOGY

Making sense of our inner lives can be one of the most daunting of spiritual tasks. Here, with candor and precision, Joe Storr takes us on a tour of his inner life—detailing the ups and downs of his spiritual journey, and modeling a healthy way to walk with God during seasons of plenty as well as seasons of dryness.

TIM MOREY, SENIOR PASTOR
LIFE COVENANT CHURCH

To my parents, Howard and Gail.
Thank you for giving me life, and for believing in me.

TABLE OF CONTENTS

MEN NEED TO BE MEN. WE NEED TO BE MEN for our own sake, and for the sake of our families, churches, and communities. The world desperately needs us.

But I'm not sure that most of us know what it looks like to be a well-developed man, especially a well-developed Christian man. Based on my personal experience and my conversations with other men, many of us tend to see ourselves as "guys" only. We are uncomfortable identifying ourselves as men. Some I have spoken with feel that the title of "man" belongs to their fathers—yet these men are fathers themselves. Part of the reason for this prevalent "guy" self-descriptor must be the pervasive use of the word among speakers of the English language.[1] We have been conditioned to some degree by our culture to see ourselves as *guys* and not men. However, I believe there is also an internal reason why we do this.

---

1   It makes sense that "guy" would be so widely used. The word enables us to communicate well and easily without making laborious and sometimes awkward distinctions. For example, "guys" can refer to old men, younger men, and adolescents as well. It can even extend beyond reference to males and embrace females. According to Eugene Volokh, writing for the Washington Post, the word likely originated in the early 1600s as a disparaging term. Some speculate that the descriptor didn't become widely used as a generic, non-disparaging term until the early 1800s. Therefore, its use is a relatively recent phenomenon. For thousands of years of human history, "guys" was simply not used.

As I look at the landscape of Christian masculinity across both the church and para-church organizations, I notice that there is something missing in our discussions and in our literature. *We don't seem to know what to do with our brokenness*—our sin, dysfunction, immaturity, wounds, failure, guilt, shame, anger, sadness, and all the rest. Sure, there are organizations and authors who do their part to cast a vision of biblical manhood and help men enter into this vision. They offer good teaching, and they rally men to build community, share their lives, and receive prayer, encouragement, and accountability for the journey. This is very good. My own father's life was radically changed through the ministry of Promise Keepers, for example. However, as Dr. John Coe, my seminary professor, used to say, we tend to focus on putting on the "new man" in Ephesians 4:24 and only superficially put off the "old man" in Ephesians 4:22.[2] For example, we may try to ignore our brokenness altogether, minimize it, pray "quick" prayers asking God to take away what we see, or simply resolve to be different.

The church, in particular, can also be a confusing place for men because it doesn't tend to hold up a clear and compelling image of fully-orbed, biblical masculinity. The church doesn't have much to say about our brokenness other than (1) it shouldn't be there or (2) we should be able to keep it under control, whatever it is. Rather, the church is a place where a lot of men feel emasculated.

I get it. In fact, there was a time in my journey with Jesus when the church—and most of Christianity—felt emasculating. My church experience included much exhortation in the fruit of the Spirit:

---

2   Dr. John Coe is the Director of the Institute for Spiritual Formation, Talbot School of Theology, La Mirada, CA.

> But the fruit of the Spirit is love, joy, peace, patience, kindness, goodness, faithfulness, gentleness, self-control.
>
> —Galatians 5:22-23a

These are wonderful qualities, of course. However, they sometimes felt annihilating to me, like I had to shut down parts of myself to become a man whose life could be characterized by patience, kindness, and gentleness, for example. What about the part of me that longed for something that felt more robust? I wanted adventure; I wanted to be on an important mission full of challenge and maybe danger, too. I blamed the church for trying to "minimize" me in its mission to produce "kind" men.

However, I now see that the true source of my irritation was not the church alone, but my own heart and understanding. To be authentic men, we have to be whole men, not only "strong" men. *All* parts of our character—including the weaknesses of our hearts—have to be brought under Jesus' reign and influence. I was weak in the fruit of the Spirit. There were things in my character—anger, lust, insecurity, immaturity, self-centeredness, fear, wounds, sadness, etc.—that opposed my growth in Christlikeness. To be whole, I had to explore these parts of my character with Jesus and try to understand them. Unexpectedly, the path to more authentic manhood would pass directly through my weakness and brokenness.

Our culture does not value brokenness. We tend to wince at verses like these:

> For you will not delight in sacrifice, or I would give it; you will not be pleased with a burnt offering. The sacrifices

of God are a broken spirit; a broken and contrite heart,
O God, you will not despise.

—Psalm 51:16-17

Blessed are the poor in spirit, for theirs is the kingdom
of heaven.

—Matthew 5:3

Rather than embrace the sort of weakness we see in these
verses and others like them, our culture elevates strength.
Generally, we are taught to discover our strengths and exploit
them to the fullest. On the other hand, our weaknesses are
to be hidden, overcome, or shored up so they do not become
liabilities in the exercise of our strengths.

There is some wisdom in this emphasis on strength. After all, we have to make our way in the world. However, I'm
concerned that this focus on strength could also leave us as
incomplete men. We might lack deep substance as persons—
we might become mere shadows of what we could be, leaving
large parts of ourselves underdeveloped. More than a few of
us may even feel like adolescent boys walking around in the
bodies of men. The way to fuller manhood is obedience to
God in the Scriptures. And the Scriptures command humility:

He has told you, O man, what is good; and what does the
Lord require of you but to do justice, and to love kindness,
and to walk humbly with your God?

—Micah 6:8

To be humble is to be free from pride or arrogance, free
from inflation of any kind. Humility demands, then, that we

accept the whole truth about ourselves—both our strengths and our weaknesses. This means that we must allow God to examine our hearts, and we must be willing to accept whatever He shows us (Psalm 139:23-24). Maybe He shows us that we lack love, patience, kindness, gentleness; we might see that our anger is a real issue or our deep insecurities are the true engine behind our successes. We have to allow ourselves to be broken and dependent before God and experience our deep need for Him. Jesus' presence in our broken places, our weak places, heals and grows us into men of depth, substance, and power. This level of openness with God requires great courage, though, since we are typically afraid of our weaknesses and any acknowledgment of our need for help. Openness threatens our idealized image of ourselves, along with the acceptance, love, and respect we feel our image secures for us.

However, as men, we know what it is like to muster our courage and push through fears. We exercise courage in our relationships, jobs, commitments, responsibilities. Even some of our hobbies call upon our courage! Therefore, men, find courage now to face your weaknesses with God as well. You and your relationships will forever be changed.

I suppose, by the world's standards, I had all the markings of a man for most of my life. I was a military officer and an engineer. I flew airplanes, jumped out of airplanes, led rocket launches, and negotiated international agreements. I excelled on the Green Beret's obstacle course at Fort Bragg, North Carolina, but decided against a transfer from the Air Force to the Army. I was a track and field athlete as well—I threw the javelin until an elbow injury crushed my hopes for high-level competition. However, I always felt more like a "guy" than a man. I didn't see myself—or refer to myself—as a man. Fortunately, my experience has changed and I have finally taken my place in the world as a man. The path I took is not one that I chose for myself; I did not want it at first. Because the path to more robust manhood takes us—among other places—directly through our brokenness.

This is my story.

Through my story I attempt to do one thing: encourage men to open their brokenness to God and become—as fully as possible—who they were created to be. I try to voice this encouragement through a logical thread that builds throughout my story and is summarized in the figure below:

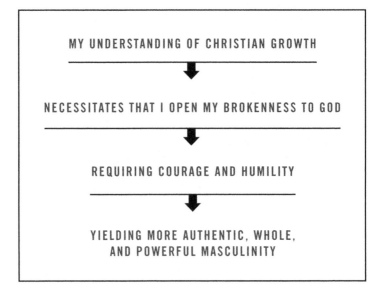

18

Each chapter along the way consists of three parts:

1. *What I was doing in the particular season of life I describe.*

2. *What God was doing in my heart during this time.* You will notice a consistent theme in God's activity in my life: He tried to draw me into a deeper, more honest, and more transformative relationship with Him through persistent invitation to share my brokenness and other parts of my heart that I had repressed.

3. *Points of connection between your story and mine, as well as questions for prayer and discussion.* These questions are designed to facilitate honest reflection, with God, about our lives and hearts. I hope that they both establish and nurture a deeply open disposition toward Him that leads to greater healing and growth.

Admittedly, God dealt with me—and I responded to Him—as an introvert. Much of the repressed material I shared with God I identified through spiritual practices like self-reflection, journaling, solitude and silence, and retreat. However, as I point out in Chapter 8, you don't have to be an introvert or engage in these types of practices to identify suppressed content. God uses many ways to show us what we need to see and share with Him (Romans 8:28-29). For example, He might use Scripture, our circumstances, trials, and other people to expose things we have buried inside. I have often noticed how effectively God uses relationships, in particular, to break open hidden parts of ourselves. I once talked with a man who felt that his sanctification actually *began* on his wedding day!

Finally, I conclude this book with an appendix that addresses potential questions or concerns some evangelicals hold about taking the time to look at our own hearts. Some conservative evangelicals, in particular, hold thoughtful reservations about spending too much time in self-examination. I have tried to include top-level answers to the most common questions and concerns I have encountered (being a conservative evangelical myself).

I realize that Christian masculinity is the subject of an ongoing discussion with many helpful voices. I am a single voice adding my perspective to one dimension of this conversation. I am not trying to discuss comprehensive biblical masculinity. The span of fully-orbed manhood is well beyond the scope of this book. Also, I am not a husband or father—I do not have the family experience that is common to the vast majority of men. Yet, my journey with Jesus has given me something to say about a key aspect of our development as masculine souls: brokenness. I pray that you will receive my words with an open and courageous heart.

1

AIRPLANES, PARACHUTES, AND PERSONAL TRIALS

FOUR YEARS OF MY LIFE USED TO FEEL LIKE a lot of time. Now, looking back, those 1,460 days that once stretched out before me in Dayton, Ohio feel like a muzzle flash. The time collapses into a small segment of a long linear life map with a punchy title above it. For the four years I spent at Wright-Patterson Air Force Base, that title reads, "Crucible."

Not that it was all bad. I don't think it was. I fell in love while I was stationed there and spent nearly every vacation chasing my girlfriend all over the country. She lived in New Jersey, then California, then Georgia. I flew and drove the equivalent of an entire lap around the planet to be with her. She was very pretty and loved life. At the faintest hint of adventure or fun, her eyes flashed, revealing a captivating inner light. I hope she is still loving her life.

I built some lasting friendships in Ohio, too. And before I left, God saved me. As I said, good things happened in that time! But the label "Crucible" still fits because my inner world was in turmoil during those four years. When I remember that time, I still feel the disorienting chaos of my thought life and the extreme tension I carried in my body.

I arrived on base a brand-new second lieutenant, fresh from the Aerospace Engineering program and ROTC at Georgia Tech. Because I did well at Georgia Tech, I was assigned to the Wright Laboratory, where I could use my education to do research for the Air Force. I was fortunate; I asked for this assignment and I got it.

Our job was to test aircraft structural materials—metals and composites—for durability and damage tolerance. We also developed analytical methods to predict the lives of these materials on aircraft performing different missions. For example, how long can an A-10 safely fly its air-to-ground role with Material X before we have to inspect for cracks in the structure and make repairs? Or, if we use a certain paint removal process on F-15s, will we affect the structural life of the aircraft in its air-to-air role? What about future aircraft that will fly faster than anything we currently have in our inventory and generate extremely high surface temperatures? What about lighter, but stronger and more durable materials?

We had big, loud machines behind glass doors that tested material samples for both strength and fatigue life. We had racks of computers to run analyses that would, hopefully, predict the outcomes of these tests. PhDs in ties and technicians in lab coats kept everything running. I did my part, too, and eventually led this group of men and women. However, the more I learned about research, the more dissociated I felt at the laboratory.

I don't believe that the Air Force should assign brand-new officers to work on technologies that may or may not see the light of day for 15 years. Or maybe I should say that the Air

Force shouldn't assign brand-new officers *like me* to do this type of work! I am a builder, a creator—I thrive on establishing things, standing things up. Movement is key to my happiness. But wheels turn slowly in research; it is painstakingly detailed work. Since one of my strengths found in StrengthsFinder© is "Strategic," I fully embrace the critical importance of research. I just think it's best if someone else does it. The research culture is not a good fit with my personality.

Our commander tried to keep us all inspired, even when our research was not yielding fruitful results. He once got philosophical with me and explained the essential nature of research and the unknown outcome of any particular line of inquiry. He said, and I know he was right, that failures in research are vitally important, just as the successes are. Failures show us what will not work and why—they propel the state-of-the-art forward. Well, *that* sucks.

PERSONAL CRISIS

Since my professional life was not engrossing, it didn't do much to take the edge off of my personal problems. My private challenges were many, but a single phrase captures them well: I was in existential crisis.

I was an Air Force officer before I was a Christian. I did my best to look the part of an imposing military man—sharp, confident, competent, and dedicated—but my inner world was so different, so chaotic. Intense anxiety saturated my time away from work. Oppressive questions and dark apprehension riddled my thought life and threatened to unhinge my equilibrium: Why are we humans so different from every other creature on Earth? Why are we the only animals that seem to have the capacity to contemplate our own mortality and become disturbed by this awareness? Is there anything in the world—or anywhere else for that matter—that lasts forever? Isn't it strange—and tragic—to be so high-functioning, yet finally disappear into the same nothingness that held us before birth? Does anybody love me who doesn't "have to" love me, like my parents, for example? I sure didn't mind a beer or two—or more—when these thoughts buffeted me. But, often, I felt the impulse to run from them, to shake them off.

At these times, I would get in my car and drive. The amount of concentration required to drive a car would take the edge off of my anxiety and bring my mind back to the surface of my life. Some nights I aimlessly drove around in the local area for a half-hour or so. These local drives were usually enough to distance myself from my palpable fear of going insane. On tougher nights, I would drive for hours. One night in particular, I found myself in Indianapolis before I felt comfortable turning around and heading home. I suppose that was a drive of over 300 miles.

The crushing part of this experience, this inner chaos, was that I had tried so hard for such a long time to master it. For years I attempted to be like my friend Chris from college. He was calm and at peace even when exams pressed in on us and his other responsibilities left him not-so-well prepared. He was authentic; he was mature. He wore no masks—he was comfortable and content being himself and never made much of himself in front of others. One day after class we were walking together and I had an almost irrepressible impulse to ask him a couple of potentially embarrassing questions. But I was intensely insecure in those days. Can you imagine how vulnerable I would have had to be to say, "Hey, Chris, why are you so different? How can I be like you?"

I discovered as time went by that Chris was a Christian, the first one I had met that I can remember. But I was resistant to religion. I felt, and I don't know where this came from, that religion was a crutch to help the weak deal with harsh realities. I wanted to appear strong, not weak. So I made a decision that would direct me down a futile path for the next seven years of my life: I would become like Chris, but I would get there my own way.

And so the search began—the conscious search for some degree of meaning and fulfillment that I hoped would lead me to a state of genuine peace and contentment. I sought satisfaction in every place I could think of that wasn't blatantly illegal: relationships, graduate school and the pursuit of knowledge, job success, alcohol. I even tried to build the impressive resume of an adventurer that would make me—at least in appearance—a more put-together man. I flew airplanes and got my pilot's license; I flew gliders; I did some repelling and a good bit of scuba diving. And all of this served one purpose alone: I was emptier and more scared than ever before. The questions I carried now felt even more magnified to me and more unanswerable. My anxiety soared.

There was only one thing left to do, and I did it. I called my buddy Chris. He was in New Mexico flying F-111s at the time. My part of the conversation was simple and direct and reflected my desperation: "I don't know what you have, but I know that you have what I need. Can you help me?"

My search now took a radical turn. I was actually looking for God!

Chris sent me a Bible and told me where I should start reading—in one of the Gospels, I think. And he told me that it would be good to find a church that had a solid reputation for accurately teaching the Bible. So I fumbled around looking for recommendations from people I knew who seemed to be serious church-goers. There were few. Finally, one Sunday morning, I found myself at a large Baptist church not far from my home.

DESPAIRING OF GOD

The church was huge and the parking lot stretched for acres in all directions. On the ground floor, a sweeping sanctuary opened in front of me that could easily seat 1,000 people. Above me, a balcony jutted out and loomed over the people below. People…they were everywhere! I felt completely out of place—I didn't know how a church service worked, what happened when, where I should sit. What I did know was that I wanted to be left alone. This was an experiment and I wanted to conduct it in private. I dodged peoples' glances like they were throwing heavy objects at me and found a seat way up in the last row of the balcony. Pasted to the back wall and comfortable that I was invisible, I was ready to hear what the preacher had to say.

It was infuriating!

I managed to stay through the entire sermon, but at the end I left in a hurry, feeling nothing but frustration and anger. I had been set up!

The preacher from Kentucky drew me in at first. He was a small man with a southern accent, which made me feel comfortable, being from the South myself. And he had an earthy way about him. He talked straight and used everyday words that seemed to articulate what was in my heart. I could have the character that I longed for—I could be loving, joyful, peaceful, patient, kind, and all the rest. I could have a mission in this world that made my life purposeful and fulfilling. I could live in devoted community. I was all ears—I was with him! Looking back, this sermon was meticulously designed to mirror my deepest needs and desires. Then the preacher got to the punch line, and he dropped me back into my abyss.

He said this life he had described was available to me right now, if only I would believe in Jesus' sacrifice for me and give my life to Him. Well, screw you! *Up yours* for baiting me, for telling me I could escape my inner hell and have everything I ached for, then declaring with the weight of an official proclamation that it was impossible for me. Because I didn't believe in Jesus' sacrifice for me, and I couldn't *make myself* believe something! I felt violated, betrayed, and a raw anger flared up in me that protected me from feeling utter hopelessness. For now, I could hate the preacher and not feel despair over lacking the *one* thing required of me—faith. The keys to the Kingdom were for others. God had shut me out.

Weeks passed before my temper subsided and I could pick up my Bible again. But, I did...I must have felt some residue of hope. How else could I have had any desire to read the Word? And, as Providence would have it, I turned to Matthew 7:7-8:

> Ask, and it will be given to you; seek, and you will find; knock, and it will be opened to you. For everyone who asks receives, and the one who seeks finds, and to the one who knocks it will be opened.

These verses spawned a weighty idea: I would ask God to give me what I lacked. I would pray to God for the first time in my life, and I would ask Him a life-or-death question.

APPROACHING GOD

Two things stand out to me about the night I first talked with God. One, I was calm, which for me was completely out of the ordinary. Clusters of intense thoughts usually filled my mind, both the product of my anxiety and the fuel that fed it. But the simplicity of a single, compelling question concentrated my thoughts and quieted my ruminations. Two, I was honest. I articulated my heart without filters or interpretations. In a word, I was *present*. The authentic me was talking with the real God.

My prayer rose up from a deep place inside me: "God, if You are who I think You are, then You know I don't believe in Jesus. But, You know that I *want* to believe. If I somehow do my part—if I ask and seek and knock—will You make sure I find You?"

I wouldn't talk with God again for months. Instead, I focused on doing my part. I kept reading my Bible, and I went back to the church I stormed out of. I listened carefully to the sermons. My posture was one of receptivity. I was a hungry man needing someone to feed me; I was a student needing to be taught. I was dependent. And I don't remember having any big questions that demanded answers. There was no cognitive formula: "God, if You would help me understand this historical debate or that moral issue, I would be able to believe." I just kept showing up for my Bible reading and for church.

The only explanation I have for what happened next is from Ephesians 2:8-9 (emphasis mine):

> For by grace you have been saved through faith. And this is not your own doing; it is the *gift of God*, not a result of works, so that no one may boast.

One day—six months or so after I prayed—I became aware that I believed! Not a light switch moment; I hadn't toggled from 100 percent disbelief to 100 percent belief. More like the gradual change of a dimmer switch. But Jesus, His lordship, and His death and resurrection were more real to me than before. Somehow, God gifted me a measure of faith. Was it enough to give my life to Him? Not yet. But it was something!

Only a little more time passed before I felt the confidence of Romans 10:9:

> Because, if you confess with your mouth that Jesus is Lord and believe in your heart that God raised him from the dead, you will be saved.

I believed. Would I confess? My journey toward faith now entered an entirely different phase. I no longer needed to believe. Now, I needed to choose. Would I give my life to God in Christ, or would I live apart from Him?

A terrible battle began to rage within me. When I moved towards the choice for God, I became paralyzed by the gravity of the decision, how momentous it was. I would be giving my life to someone else! I would live under God's authority and submit to His ways. Everything would be different for the rest of my life. There would be no going back to living on my own and for myself. When I moved towards the choice of autonomy, on the other hand, I was tormented by darkness, fear, and loneliness. The tension felt excruciating. I couldn't move. I needed a "forcing function" to thrust me toward God. And I got it.

A couple of friends and I wanted to take advantage of a program between the Air Force and the Army that offered "service familiarization" opportunities. What this meant was that selected personnel from the Air Force would spend some time with the Army—and vice-versa—in one of their training programs. The theory stipulated that familiarization with sister services would enhance mutual understanding and joint operations. My friends and I decided we would apply for the program and, specifically, see if we couldn't get ourselves killed.

Airborne School is the Army's elite paratrooper training program at Fort Benning, Georgia. The program is three weeks long, and it is the entryway into the famed airborne units that have played pivotal roles in battles since World War II. So, as you might expect, the Army is very serious about the training. I would come to appreciate this.

"Why not?" my friend challenged me.

"I don't know…we might die?" I replied.

"Oh, come on," he continued. "And hey, let's go in August!"

"You mean, like in the *summer?*" I asked with unmasked incredulity. He was from New England, and I wasn't sure he appreciated how hot it can get in southern Georgia. "It's nearly 100 degrees down there in August!" I protested.

I can still see my friend, charged with the raw excitement that comes from the most comprehensive naïveté. I don't know what he said next or what I was thinking, but he won the day. We applied, and we got in!

As our training date approached, I worked out hard. By the time I headed to Fort Benning, I was doing hundreds of pushups and sit-ups every day, and I could run two miles in just over 12 minutes. I was ready. But, spiritually, I wasn't prepared to go. The thought of dying in some unfortunate accident haunted me. So, finally, I settled the matter. One night before I left home for Fort Benning, I determined that I would ask Jesus to save me and come into my heart to be with me and shepherd me.

I knelt down on the floor in my living room and started to pray. But I couldn't bring myself to give my life to Jesus. I could form the words in my mind, but I couldn't say them. I couldn't get them out. The momentousness of what I was doing was heavy on me. There was a literal battle raging for my soul—I was thrown one way, then the other. There came a point when I just didn't think I would be able to do it. Then, an added measure of resolve somehow came to me, and I pushed—I forced—the words out of my mouth! Having heaved the words to God that saved me, I collapsed on the floor and lay there a while. It was finished. If I punched a hole in the ground during training, I would be with God forever.

THE PROVIDENCE OF GOD

I woke to the muffled sound of an instructor screaming at me. He was standing squarely in front of me looking very imposing and very angry. But whatever he was saying was difficult to make out at first. I was a little groggy and the roar of the C-141 Starlifter's four jet engines didn't help. Then I caught it: "What are you doing sleeping?! Are you stupid or something? You're about to jump out of a @#$!ing airplane for God's sake!"

Good point. It wasn't the best time to take a nap. I would later learn that I had a sinus infection during my last week of training, and my illness, along with the oppressive heat, sapped my energy. I got myself squared away and convinced the instructor that I was coherent. All I had to do now was haul myself to the door with all of the other troops in my "stick" and make my final jump. Training was over—we would graduate the next day.

I made it through without the terrible accident I had feared. I came closer than I would've liked, though. During my third jump, I had a parachute malfunction that easily could've put me in the hospital or the morgue. Everything started out "textbook" on that jump. We checked our gear, loaded up, and settled in for the short ride to the drop zone. We were warned, as usual, when we were 10 minutes out. Then, we were told to "stand up and hook up!" We immediately stood and hooked our static lines to the long steel cable that would fly away with the C-130 Hercules aircraft and pull our parachutes. Then, green light! The command to "GO!" I exited the aircraft in a tuck position and plunged through the prop wash toward the earth as I counted to four: *One one thousand, two one thousand…* then the violent jerk upward as the chute filled with air. So far, so good.

The first thing we were taught to do once the parachute deployed was to quickly look up to inspect the canopy. If there were no anomalies, we would ride the rig to the ground. If there was a serious problem, we immediately pulled the reserve. Since we were jumping at only 1,250 feet, there wasn't time for deliberation.

I looked up and saw small, scattered patches of sky shining through my canopy—there were holes in my chute! One of the risers had ridden over the top of the canopy during deployment and burned away some of the material. No worries yet—I obediently looked at the other jumpers in the sky to gauge my rate of descent. Was I falling faster than they were? Should I pull my reserve? I decided that all was well and left the reserve alone. Our instructors told us that maneuvering was very difficult with both the main chute and the reserve deployed, and landings were particularly hard. I opted to ride what I had. I had no idea that I was in real danger.

Depth perception is harder when higher aloft, so I didn't get any immediate feedback that would bring my decision not to pull my reserve into question. But the closer I got to the ground, the faster the ground rushed towards me—violently, impassively. I was falling FAST; I was rocked with terror! I knew that I was about to get seriously injured—my legs, my back. Some part of my body was going to be horribly mangled. I braced for the worst and tried to focus on executing the best and quickest landing roll I possibly could. I felt helpless to change whatever was going to happen, except for that landing roll. I only hoped that I wasn't falling so fast that it would be impossible to roll when my feet hit the ground.

Just when I expected to slam into the earth—SQUISH! I landed like I had floated onto a huge pillow. I was fine! The terror that had flooded my body slowly dissipated with each beat of my pounding heart. I wanted to lie there in profound relief and not move until I could decide whether to laugh or cry. As it turned out, I had found the only part of the huge Alabama landing zone that had retained water from earlier rains. A mud puddle the size of a semi truck providentially received and enveloped me.

I had gathered my chute and stuffed it into its bag by the time another jumper landed next to me. It was a soldier only two places behind me in my stick! He said, "Dude, you were falling like a damn rock!" I still feel some residue of the terror and relief I felt in those fateful few seconds in Alabama. I'm so grateful to God for sparing me some horrific injury, or worse.

Trust is everything. To execute those jumps at Airborne School, I had to *make* myself leap from the airplane when my heart—then in my throat—was screaming, "NO!" What enabled me to throw myself through the door was trust. I had to trust the pilots and the jumpmasters, as well as the parachute riggers and the training I had received.

I'm shocked by how substantially my time at Fort Benning mirrored the night I gave my life to Jesus. I had to "jump" that night—I had to trust that Jesus would rescue me and that He intended only the best for me. And don't we have to jump again and again? Don't the circumstances of our lives continue to demand deeper and deeper trust in God along with a strong dose of courage? I mention trust and courage now because I believe that reading this book might be one of these opportunities for you to lean on God even more. We will be exploring parts of ourselves that may be hard to face. And we will be humbling ourselves before Him and asking Him to meet us in these difficult realities to love and guide us. Trusting God is essential. Bless you as we jump together.

MOVING ON

With my Army training behind me and silver wings on my chest, I drove back to Ohio. When I got to the office, I found orders to report to Los Angeles Air Force Base. My first tour was over. The day after the pastor from Kentucky baptized me in the church I once flipped off, I made my way west. I was a brand-new believer, and everything felt new.

PRAYER AND DISCUSSION

Consider these questions with God and, if possible, write down your reflections.

1. God, how did You pursue me to make me Your own? How did You come for me?

2. When did You intervene in my life to save me from something that would not be good for me?

3. I want to be more grateful, God. What are You doing in my life right now that I can appreciate more and thank You for?

4. God, am I already aware of some things in my heart that are difficult to face, things that I try to keep hidden from You and maybe myself? What makes me want to hide these things, Lord? What would it look like to trust You more with them?

2

ROCKETS AND NEW BEGINNINGS

IN THE EARLY YEARS OF MY ADULTHOOD, I WAS just doing what I thought I was supposed to do. But it looked a lot like meandering. I didn't go into life after high school with some compelling sense of purpose and a clear plan. I wasn't as "put together" as my friend Walt, who wanted to be a pilot or Joe, who loved computers and longed for the chance to be on the cutting edge of some exciting new development. In fact, nobody from our family had gone to college, so the world of universities and careers felt exotic and overwhelming. I applied to Georgia Tech because I had some interest in airplanes and because Walt said that it was a good school for aerospace engineering. I would graduate from college and be well into my first Air Force tour before I realized that Georgia Tech was better than good—it was elite. I don't know what its ranking was in the mid-1980s when I was there, but it is ranked number two today.

Our family wasn't a military family either. I found myself in ROTC because I felt the need to be part of something bigger than myself and I had a scholarship. But I didn't know the Air Force culture. I had little understanding of how assignments and promotions worked or how careers were built. I felt like I had stepped into another world with its rules, customs, and aggressive "move up or move on" personnel system. ROTC helped acclimate me to some degree, but I was still very green. And like almost all of my moves, I headed to Los Angeles having never been there and not knowing a soul.

Now I was also a brand-new Christian!

In retrospect, God chose LA to establish my faith and to grow my leadership in the church and in the Air Force. I didn't choose this move for myself. I had orders to Los Angeles before I could even call the Personnel Center and start a conversation about my next move. When I did call to see if there might be somewhere else I could go, a friendly assignments officer cheerfully reminded me that the military was not a democracy. I cheerfully passed on some words to him, too.

BELONGING

Being "born again" is not just a reference to John 3 or 1 Peter 1, it is the perfect metaphor for the experience itself. I *felt* born again! In the best possible way, my understanding of the world and everything in it had been blown up. I was in a new world now and I didn't know how to live in it. I was a child, full of naïveté. I would have to learn. The most fundamental and sincere questions occupied my mind: What do I do now? How do I live? How do I grow? How do I go about my work? What do friendships look like? Remarkably, these questions didn't seem to stress me out. They were the stuff of adventure, of discovery.

But who knows how much trouble I would've gotten into if God hadn't planted me in a church full of people who could help me. I immediately got involved in a Bible study, learned about "quiet times," and regularly attended services. I loved it! I couldn't get enough reading, prayer, sermons, community life, and service. I had energy, even zeal for all of these spiritual practices. I was a voracious learner, growing all the time in my understanding of God and the new Kingdom I lived in.

I had great friends, too. I shared a house with Mark, Matt, and Steve. Tom also joined us, along with Ray, in a group we formed to share our lives and to challenge each other to be the best men we could be. Except for Ray, our older mentor, we were all fairly new believers. I connected especially well with Mark—he was an Air Force officer who would go on to be a commander in special operations. We met every morning before work to check in with each other and to pray together. We formed a deep bond that has lasted more than 20 years—he's got my back, and I've got his. He prayed for me at the opening of my retirement ceremony in California, and I prayed at his retirement ceremony in Florida. Both occasions were marked by deep personal knowledge, respect, and love.

I also tried to reorient my life to God as I learned His ways, commands, and desires. I changed some old habits. First, I silenced my foul mouth. Actually, I think God silenced my foul mouth—I just stopped cussing! For years I seemed incapable of saying a complete sentence without burping up some expletive. I tried everything to stop, including a pact with friends to put a dollar in a jar whenever I released some obscenity. I gave away a lot of money. Nothing worked. Now, God *gifted me* a clean mouth and a clean mind, too. I no longer swore even in my thought life.

I jettisoned pornography as well. I looked at pornographic magazines for many years, and watched some videos, too. All of this material immediately found the dumpster. I continued to struggle for some time with revealing or even racy advertisements and movies, but eventually I released these forms of "soft porn," too. I'm so grateful that I never used a computer to look at women. I don't know why I didn't look on the internet, but letting go of inappropriate images would've been much harder if I had.

Finally, I let alcohol go. I was used to weekend binges, so it seemed best to release alcohol entirely until I could be sure that I wasn't misusing it. I abstained for six years, but now I enjoy a beer or two. Life got so much better after these three acts of obedience, in particular. These "structural" changes directed my life away from darkness and toward the light, and they brought tangible measures of peace and joy. I felt cleaner, lighter, and more at rest. I could breathe easier.

Work brought a lot of satisfaction, too. I had several jobs during my four years at LA Air Force Base, but the one I enjoyed most was my time as the Titan IV rocket program's Chief of Mission Design and Analysis. The Titan IV was a monster rocket, the largest launch vehicle in the Air Force inventory at the time. Its function was to lift the heaviest and most sensitive military satellites to their mission orbits. The booster was fully operational—we were launching regularly and successfully.

Our responsibilities in Mission Design and Analysis covered a lot of territory. My team of Air Force officers and independent contractors from Aerospace Corporation worked alongside Martin Marietta, the prime contractor for the Titan IV. Our job in the Air Force was to verify that the work performed by the Martin Marietta engineers was correct and yielded the required— extremely high!—probability of mission success. We evaluated vehicle trajectories and fuel usage. We calculated the load and vibration levels the rocket and satellite would experience in flight. We managed flight software development. And we positioned assets all over the globe to gather in-flight data—from portable ground stations, to aircraft, to on-orbit satellites. These assets received and recorded telemetry data from the rocket real-time for later analysis. That was another part of our duties: to collect flight data and distribute it to analysts who would make sure everything worked flawlessly before we flew our next mission. We were constantly challenged to make this post-flight data analysis process as fast as possible so we could launch more frequently.

This position earned me the nickname "rocket scientist" among my friends Mark, Matt, Steve, and Tom. I didn't seem to mind. When you're insecure, you take everything you can get. But, the truth is, I was responsible for the work of rocket scientists, but wasn't a full-fledged member of the fraternity. And in the spirit of truth-telling, I was always relieved and impressed when the rocket performed the way we predicted it would in our meetings! Given its size and the complexity of its systems and subsystems, I felt like any number of things could go wrong. And once, something did go wrong.

We were all set to launch a mission designated K-11 from Vandenberg AFB on the California coast. On top of the rocket sat a very expensive satellite that had a critically important mission. I was in the Winds Room that day, as I was for all launches. We sent up balloons carrying equipment that measured the wind speed and direction as a function of altitude. We used this data to make sure the rocket could fly its assigned trajectory for the day without inducing unacceptable loads on the vehicle, especially where the bulbous payload faring bolted to the main body. We had good wind data that day and gave our "go" for launch. When the countdown got close to liftoff, we made our way outside to watch. We were miles from the launch pad and safe, of course. But the massive engines were still gloriously loud, the plume longer than the length of the rocket and bright. Smoke was everywhere. We were on our way!

The rocket flew beautifully. Then, a puff of smoke appeared somewhere near the center of the vehicle. This was strange—there shouldn't be any emissions at this time of flight other than the contrail. We wondered at first if the solid rocket motors strapped to the core vehicle might be separating early. Maybe they were already spent. Then, all questions were removed—a quick succession of violent explosions ripped through the vehicle and spewed smoking, mangled remains in all directions. It was over. The mission failed.

A deep silence fell among us. No one spoke a word or even had a word form in his mind. As I looked around, the 20 or so engineers with me just stared blankly into the sky or toward the ground. I felt gut-shot. And since we didn't know what happened, I felt guilty. What if the accident was somehow linked to our work? What if it was ultimately my fault? I carried the weight of this possibility for many days. Not knowing...it's horrible to lose such a critical asset. It's excruciating to think that it could be your fault with no information speeding your way that could relieve your heavy fear.

When we finally gathered the flight data, it was clear that a hardware anomaly was the source of the disaster. The solid propellant in one of the strap-on boosters burned a hole through the casing and created a thrust vector away from the main body. The solid rocket motor was literally tearing itself away from the core vehicle. The launch vehicle was armed with ordnance for just such a scenario—the Inadvertent Separation Destruct System fired and destroyed the entire rocket before it could scatter under thrust in unknown directions and wreak untold damage.

Our team was off the hook and the dark cloud that oppressed me lifted. But a pall settled over the program as we worked to get back to normal operations. A somber environment sapped our morale. The energy and optimism that once characterized our people—the sound of positive voices and the bustle of busy movement—gave way to slow, quiet motion and reserved speech. It would be a year before we could put it all behind us.

SOMETHING IS OFF

About this time, I also received "data" showing a potential malfunction in my spiritual life. I had grown fast in my first few years as a Christian. I was in a very supportive, Word-centered community, and I had my close friends walking with me. My first-ever Bible study was far behind me now, that study where I scrambled through the index of my Bible to find 1 Corinthians and catch up with the others who were already talking about the text. I now led studies myself and would soon be asked to join the leadership team for our 300-member congregation. But something wasn't quite right.

I remember in detail the day I first started to question how the Christian life is supposed to operate. I was at home on a typical LA Saturday morning—sunny and moderately warm, without a cloud in the sky. Best weather in the world! I sat in my sunlit dining room enjoying some strong coffee and a slow start to my day. I was reading Galatians, chapter 5. Then, as I glanced up to look at the tree just outside the sliding glass doors, I had a "Hebrews 4:12 moment." While I was thinking about the Word, the Spirit helped me notice my reaction to Galatians 5 and invited me into an important conversation with God. Until this day, I hadn't understood the fullness of Hebrews 4:12:

> For the word of God is living and active, sharper than any two-edged sword, piercing to the division of soul and spirit, of joints and of marrow, and discerning the thoughts and intentions of the heart.

This verse in Hebrews opened an entirely new dimension of my relationship with God. Certainly we read the Word and apply what we learn with the help of the Spirit; this is part of putting on the new man, as spoken of in Ephesians 4:24. But, Hebrews 4:12 tells us that we not only read the Word, the Word also exposes the truth of our hearts. Through the verses I was reading in Galatians, in particular, God revealed something to me about myself: I was hiding something. And He wanted to talk with me about it (Psalm 139:23-24).

I was in Galatians 5:22-23:

> But the fruit of the Spirit is love, joy, peace, patience, kindness, goodness, faithfulness, gentleness, self-control; against such things there is no law.

As I read these verses, I felt like I was pushing down some truth about myself. I wasn't being honest. I didn't know what I might be hiding; I only knew that I felt uncomfortable and threatened. I wanted to continue reading and move past the passage, but glossing over it this way felt false to me. I reluctantly decided to stay with Galatians 5:22-23 and let God show me whatever He wanted to open to me. And He did. I was overtaken by a sudden "episode of honesty": I was not growing in the fruit of the Spirit.

After several years of being a devoted believer, I realized that I was not making significant progress toward Christlikeness. I was much more self-centered than genuinely loving, much more worried and burdened than joyful, much more anxious and fearful than at peace. My apparent lack of growth didn't seem to be a matter of unrealistic expectations or perfectionism; objectively speaking, I was not very far along. And I felt stuck. Sure, I could choose to behave in ways that appeared more loving, joyful, and peaceful, and there was some good in this behavioral change. However, I wasn't actually more loving, joyful, or peaceful from the heart.

It took some effort to accept my dismal growth in the fruit of the Spirit that Saturday morning. I had the urge to push down the truth and press into my day, to leave it behind. I was disoriented and uneasy. I didn't want this lack of love, joy, and peace to be true about me, but it was. I wanted to know what to do, but I didn't. I thought for a while about a path forward. However, I had no idea how to live the Christian life any differently than I had been. My church and my friends were all on the same path as I was. I don't remember any of us talking about our understanding of Christian development, but a theology of growth had somehow settled into my heart and my mind. It looked something like this:

1. I should be grateful for what Jesus did for me when He died on the cross.

2. I express my gratitude through obedience to God's Word. I want to be the kind of man God wants me to be and live the "set-apart" life He requires of me.

3. I work diligently in my spiritual practices (Bible reading, prayer, worship, service, etc.) and try to obey God in all things. As I do, the Holy Spirit changes me on the inside to be the kind of man who obeys from the heart and exhibits the fruit of the Spirit.

4. I change to the degree I put forth effort in my spiritual practices and in obedience.

This four-point approach to Christian maturity was all I had to work with in solving my problem of stunted growth. Years would pass before I understood that a critical part of my theology of growth was not biblical. For now, this path of development was my full understanding, and Point 4 in particular—work diligently in my spiritual practices and in obedience—grabbed me. So, after thinking for a while, I made a conscious decision: I would *try harder*. I would read more, pray more, and try to be more obedient to the Word. I would try harder to be more loving, joyful, and peaceful. The Holy Spirit, I trusted, would help me fulfill this intention and change me on the inside.

THE GROWTH GAP

This is what most of us seem to do—try harder—when we first run into what Dr. John Coe calls the Sanctification Gap or Growth Gap[3]. Of course, I didn't know about the Growth Gap at the time. And I didn't know Dr. Coe, who would later become a spiritual mentor to me, as well as my boss and friend.

---

3   Information Session, Institute for Spiritual Formation, Talbot School of Theology, La Mirada, CA, February 2008.

It was 12 years after first running into the Gap that I attended an information session for a seminary program that caught my attention. Dr. Coe spoke at the meeting, and he drew this picture on the white board:

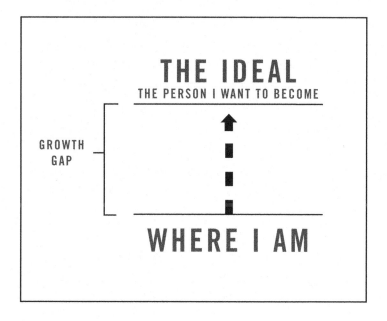

The figure shows the difference, or the gap, between the "Ideal" and where we think we are. The ideal is the description of the Christian life contained in the Word of God and in good preaching; it captures the kind of person we believe we should become. Theologians refer to this gap as the Growth Gap, and we tend to locate ourselves differently and experience our "gap" differently at various stages of our Christian journeys.

According to Dr. Coe, those of us who feel somewhat dissatisfied with where we are in our Christian journey might find ourselves somewhere on the spectrum below:

1. *Questioning how the Christian life works.* The way we have followed Jesus hasn't produced the character growth and life experience we anticipated. So, how does the Christian life truly work?

2. *Concerned about our experience of the Christian life and what our experience means.* We might feel that we are doing something wrong, or that God doesn't love us as much as others who don't seem to be wrestling with questions about their relationship with Him.

3. *Frustrated.* We could feel angry that our sincere attempts to live biblically have left us with the same struggles we have always had, yet without any idea of how to live the Christian life differently.

4. *Maybe acting out.* We may vent our frustrations in a secret life of sin—pornography, excessive drinking, fits of anger at home, etc.

5. *Disillusioned and resigned.* We simply accept that our current experience of the Christian life is all there is, and we let go of the life in Christ we once hoped for.

Coe went on to explain that we didn't always feel dissatisfied with our journey with Jesus. We likely began our walk with Him full of gratitude, hope, and deep devotion. We were thankful that He paid for our sins when He died on the cross, and we genuinely wanted to live the set-apart lives He desires for us and become the kind of men He wants us to be. We were excited to learn and grow. Spiritual practices like Scripture reading, prayer, listening to sermons, and worship delighted us, and we felt anticipation and joy when we engaged in them. We believed that if we put solid effort into these practices, our lives and characters would change in proportion to our efforts and line up with the Christian life portrayed for us in

Scripture. And we likely saw a lot of growth as we reoriented our lives to God and worked on structural and behavioral change. Then, at some point, we began to realize that we were not growing much anymore. Maybe we felt like we had hit a wall of some kind, and over time, we started to have questions.

Dr. Coe was telling my story as if he had been reading my personal email! By the time I attended the information session, I had experienced the first three reactions he outlined on the board. But, the first time I had a brush with the Growth Gap—in LA—I experienced only the first reaction he described: questioning how the Christian life really worked. I recognized that I had grown a lot in my knowledge of the Word and in obedience. My life was so much better since I made the structural changes I mentioned earlier (when I stopped cussing, drinking, and looking at pornography). I was also immersed in a life-giving community and close friendships, and I regularly heard and read the Word and tried to apply it to my life. But, was I becoming a better man, or was I just the same man doing different things?

What I mean is, I behaved differently than I had before and I experienced the benefits of this behavioral change. But was I becoming the kind of man who was more loving, joyful, peaceful, patient, kind, good, and self-controlled from the heart? Was I different, or merely acting different?

I felt that the "inside me" wasn't so different from the "me" I started my Christian journey with. But, not knowing what else to do, and feeling like I understood the importance of perseverance, I decided to try harder and hope that everything would work out. This decision set the trajectory for the next three years of my life. At the end of those three years, I would bump up against this Growth Gap again, only that time it would feel as though I had hit a wall.

With many years of ministry now under my belt, I can safely say that I was not alone. Most men I've talked with share the same experience: they are not where they feel they should be and they don't know why. They are confused, frustrated, and often feel guilty, ashamed, and internally isolated. They don't know what to do. Maybe this is where you are right now. If you are, I have just two recommendations for you at this point in our journey together. First, remember often that you are in good company—you are not the only one feeling the way you do. Second, share it all with God (Psalm 62:8). Tell Him what you are going through. Don't go it alone. Don't simply try harder. Look at your experience of the Growth Gap as an invitation to a deeper conversation with your Father. The "Prayer and Discussion" section at the end of each chapter is designed to help facilitate this open engagement with Him. Later in the book, we will examine why truth-telling is so important in our relationship with God. For now, simply try to be as honest as you can.

LEAVING LA

Almost simultaneous with my uninformed decision to try harder in the Christian life, I received orders to report back to Wright-Patterson Air Force Base, Ohio. In this stage of my career, I needed staff experience to move up the ranks. So, I reported to Headquarters, Air Force Materiel Command, the command responsible for acquisition of the Air Force's weapon systems. I was assigned to the Science and Technology Directorate, which led all Air Force research and ensured that future U.S. weapon systems maintained technological and functional superiority over projected enemy threats.

I made the drive to Ohio with my brother, and I was glad to have him with me. Leaving my new friends and church in LA was so difficult for me, and I needed my lifelong friend, my brother, to steady me. I had grown very close to my new friends, and the thought of being away from them and not knowing when I would see them again was excruciating. I felt like saying goodbye to them was a type of death. The life we had together would never be the same—it was over. What a terrific loss. I can still feel the depth of my sadness as I drove away. If not for Glenn sitting next to me, I would've pulled over and come unglued. When I got to Ohio and was alone, I cried hard as some of the pain started to flow out of me.

PRAYER AND DISCUSSION

Consider these questions with God and, if possible, write down your reflections.

1. God, what is my theology of growth? What is my belief about how You develop me, mature me?

2. Where do I locate myself on the figure showing the Growth Gap? How near or far am I from the ideal?

3. How do I feel about where I am? Do I feel good about it? Am I questioning how the Christian life works? Am I concerned, frustrated, acting out, or resigned?

4. What is it like to share my heart this way with You, God? Is it comfortable? Difficult? If it is difficult, what makes it hard?

5. God, help me to simply accept where I am right now with You in a posture of humility and openness.

3

MOVING UP AND HITTING WALLS

I **'M BACK TO THINKING ABOUT LABELS AGAIN.** How would I label the next three years I spent at Wright-Patt? Maybe something like "Reality Check." Here I faced the reality that I was on the wrong career path. And here I faced the reality that my spiritual life didn't work. But these truths didn't hit me right away. My first couple of years at my new post seemed to be taking me somewhere, both in the Air Force and in the church.

I was assigned to the International Affairs Division of the Research and Technology Directorate, Air Force Materiel Command. There I orchestrated our cooperative research efforts with Sweden. And—I still don't know how this happened—I was almost immediately named Special Assistant to the Air Force Materiel Command's Chief Scientist in his role as US National Delegate to the NATO Research and Technology Board and the NATO Air Force Armaments Group. Did they think I was somebody else?

I didn't push back, of course. I knew that the US Delegate regularly attended meetings in places like Brussels and Paris, and he met with very interesting people. So, I settled in and gave it my best shot. Primarily, I worked with an officer in the Pentagon to generate massive "Brain Books." These books were three-ring binders that prepared the boss, Dr. Don Daniels, for all of the issues that would be discussed and decided upon during upcoming meetings. I don't feel like I made a significant contribution in this role, other than packaging my partner's insights to make them easier for the boss to quickly metabolize. I knew Dr. Daniels' needs; my partner knew the issues. So, our collaboration was a success. And I did get a couple of overseas trips out of the deal.

At the same time, the job gave me face time with the Chief Scientist. So, when the Air Force consolidated all of its research efforts into a single organization—the Air Force Research Laboratory (AFRL)—and named Dr. Daniels its first Executive Director, he asked me to be his Military Assistant. I felt honored, of course, but a little cautious, too. The job was a "burnout" job. The assignment was designed to be only one year long and for a good reason. You worked all hours of the day and night and, just before you collapsed from exhaustion, you were thrown back into a normal position to recover and, hopefully, contribute. I had to think about it. My pastor had just asked me to build a small group ministry for all of the single men and women at my new church, and I wanted to be able to fulfill my commitment to him. I consulted with friends and family, then made my decision: I would take the job. I felt I could deliver in my new role and still fulfill my responsibilities at the church.

Air Force leaders formed the new Research Laboratory by aligning specialized labs all over the country under one commander and executive director. There were scientists and engineers working on space technologies in New Mexico;

armaments in Florida; human effectiveness in Texas; materials, structures, sensors, and lots of other things in Ohio. In Washington D.C., researchers focused on "basic" research that wasn't yet attached to a particular application. The 6,500-person lab was massive, and it wobbled a little as it stood up. Organizational structures had to be figured out; leaders had to be named to newly created positions. The Executive Director was at the epicenter of all this work, and I learned a ton.

Essentially, I had one job—to make sure that every issue, every question, *everything* that reached Dr. Daniels was an executive-level matter. I farmed out all other items to members of the 100-person AFRL staff. Every day I did this. Dr. Daniels came to work early in the morning and expected three things: good coffee, an email inbox on his computer screen that had already been culled of issues that he didn't need to give himself to, and a prioritized stack of paperwork on his desk with any highlights or notes I wanted to make to ease his navigation. I also made sure he was prepared for meetings, and I wrote any briefings or speeches he had to give.

I loved it. I loved the perks, too, like the Air Force business jets that took us wherever he needed to go. But I paid for it—I didn't take very good care of myself that year. Occasionally, my insecurity and people-pleasing drove me to ridiculous sacrifices. One night before heading to DC for an important meeting, I was horribly sick. I didn't sleep at all—liquids flowed from every orifice, and I was dehydrated. So, I went to the hospital, had them pump me full of intravenous fluids, then got on the plane and worked a 16-hour day in DC! I felt a little heroic when the boss noticed how bad I looked and asked if anything was wrong. Turns out he wasn't so impressed with my tenacity as he was with my stupidity. He simply asked, "What did you do that for?!" I guess it was kind of dumb.

VOCATIONAL DESERT

By the time the year was over, the lab was running smoothly and the small group ministry at church was in place with trained leaders. Everything worked out. But I was exhausted. When asked where I wanted to work next, I didn't have a quick answer. I had one year left at Wright-Patt, and I could go anywhere on base I wanted. I finally chose something that looked good for me career-wise. I moved to the Space Sector of the AFRL staff to help marry emerging technologies with future warfighter needs. I thought that maintaining the "space" theme in my career would lead me to more responsible space-related jobs. I can't say that I was enamored with space. I was just more interested in space than in any other area of work. That's not saying much, though. If I were to quantify my interest, it was probably somewhere around a 5 out of 10. Not surprisingly, then, my decision to work in the Space Sector took me into a vocational desert.

Nothing about that job grabbed me, captured me, excited me. I floundered, and I dropped a ball or two along the way. Maybe it was partly due to my exhaustion, and partly due to lack of interest and clearly defined expectations, but I felt a malaise that was difficult to penetrate and I lacked the energy to try very hard. I got by. And I felt that others in the sector were getting by, too. I'm not sure we had the right people in those jobs, myself included. Maybe my biggest contribution during my last year on base came when I told the Chief of Planning that he needed to get different people in there. I'm sure, as I retell it now, that the intervening years have rubbed away from my memory some of the nuance that fairness demands. We all brought some good things to our jobs, especially our boss at the time. But, in general, a good housecleaning was in order.

I didn't excel in my last job at Wright-Patt, but I didn't do anything to hurt my career either. I was still on track for advancement. I was selected to attend Defense Systems Management College (DSMC) at Fort Belvoir, Virginia. The college prepared promising leaders to manage large defense acquisition programs, like airplanes, rockets, and satellites. It was the best next step toward higher-level jobs in these types of programs. I was also scheduled to audition for an Air Staff position at the Pentagon. The Pentagon job would give me a top-level perspective of the type of program I would hopefully help manage one day. With a slot to attend DSMC in hand and gears turning toward a follow-on Air Staff billet, I was all set.

I couldn't help noticing, though, that somewhere deep inside I didn't really want DSMC or an Air Staff position. And I didn't seem to want whatever jobs waited on the other side of these assignments either. The path before me seemed incongruent with who I was, and I was afraid that I would "go through the motions" to get my work done without feeling any genuine interest or passion for my duties. I felt like I was on a raft floating down a river toward some town where I would live. My course was set and I was moving, but my heart just wasn't in it. I kept thinking of the possibility of other rafts and rivers and towns.

About this time, I took the Myers-Briggs personality test. This was my boss' idea, and it was a good one. I think he knew that some of us in the Space Sector weren't getting along particularly well. Understanding our unique strengths and weaknesses might help bring perspective and appreciation where frustration seemed to be prevalent. I was frustrated by a couple of teammates who took forever to make decisions. They had to tease out every conceivable angle to a problem and were very reluctant to commit to a course of action until forced to do so. They appeared to be oblivious to deadlines. On the other hand, I'm sure they were frustrated with my extreme sensitivity to time constraints and my belief in the virtue of simply making up your mind! I must admit, the test enlightened me. I came to see and appreciate the unique contributions these teammates were making. It was clear that—more often than not—we proposed better solutions to problems because they couldn't help picking at them more than the rest of us cared to.

But something more profound struck me about these test results. My personality type was very different from the rest of the team. If I ever needed objective data to validate my faint suspicion that the Air Force might not be the best fit for me, this could be it. So, I decided to meet with a Christian therapist and process the results. He didn't waste any time. The first morning I sat down with him, he immediately asked me a simple and very direct question: "What are you doing in the military?"

Turned out, I was an INFJ on the Meyers-Briggs test. What this meant was that I was a strong "feeler" and highly intuitive. I was wired for deep conversations with people. I was made to understand how they ticked and support them in their quest to become the men and women they were made to be. Something like a counselor is a good fit for an INFJ. Also, my type made up less than one percent of the population; it was the rarest of all personality types! So, fitting in practically anywhere was going to be a bit of a problem. But the military, in particular, was something of a cross-cultural experience.

"What about diplomacy?" I asked. "Would that be a fit?" Turns out, it likely would be a fit.

Interesting...because only days before this enlightening meeting with the therapist, I'd noticed some job openings for Air Attachés in our embassies overseas. I was particularly drawn to the opening in Kazakhstan because this Central Asian country was the focus of our missionary efforts at the church I attended in California. On a whim, I'd sent a message to the Personnel Center inquiring about qualifications. I hadn't heard back yet.

THIS DOESN'T WORK

On a Sunday afternoon, I boarded a plane for DC where I would "shadow" an Air Staff officer in the Pentagon. I would try on his job for a week, and the organization would try me on. The job was in the Office of the Deputy Assistant Secretary of the Air Force for Science and Technology. If everything worked out, I would take the position at the same time Dr. Daniels became the new Deputy Assistant Secretary. But, first, I had to like the job and impress the decision makers.

The officer I shadowed in the Pentagon let me do as much as I could without creating some terrible mess that would get him in trouble. I don't remember much about the issues we worked, but I do remember not liking it. I liked working with the people we encountered well enough, as well as the fast pace. We constantly toggled from one issue to another, and I enjoyed the satisfaction of getting a lot done. But the subject matter was not compelling. It wasn't interesting to me. When I watched others in the office, I noticed that they were interested in the details of the issues they were engaged with. I felt different, like I was on the outside looking in on a team of officers who fit their duties well. "God help me," I thought. "I have two engineering degrees and technology bores me to death."

The job was mine if I wanted it, but as I flew home and stared blankly out the window, the weight of reality was heavy on me. For the first time in my 12-year career, I thought about getting out of the Air Force. I didn't know what I would do in the civilian world. Only one thing was clear: if staying in the Air Force meant DSMC and the Pentagon, followed by another job I didn't want, I couldn't imagine staying in.

As I ruminated over my impending career crisis, another realization slowly bubbled up from the depths and started to take on a form, a shape, a conclusion. My spiritual life was not working. Maybe my acceptance of reality in my working life created some honest space that pulled the truth toward it like gravity. However it happened, the question I wrestled with in LA was back in my conscious mind and more urgent than before.

As I mentioned, I thought I understood how the Christian life worked:

1. I should be grateful for what Jesus did for me when He died on the cross.

2. I express my gratitude through obedience to God's Word. I want to be the kind of man God wants me to be and live the set-apart life He requires of me.

3. I work diligently in my spiritual practices (Bible reading, prayer, worship, service, etc.) and try to obey God in all things. As I do, the Holy Spirit changes me on

the inside to be the kind of man who obeys from the heart and exhibits the fruit of the Spirit.

4. I change to the degree I put forth effort in my spiritual practices and in obedience.

This was my theology of growth, my implicit understanding of Christian development. In LA, I realized that I had not grown the way I expected to grow. After careful thought, I concluded—as I must, given my theology—that the only way forward was to take my spiritual practices even more seriously. I would read more and "better," pray more, obey more, etc. The Holy Spirit would help me in this endeavor. And the Spirit would do something else, too—He would carry out His secret work to make me a different man, a man who was more loving, joyful, peaceful, patient, etc. from the heart.

Three years later in Ohio, I saw no real change. I was still the same man inside; I didn't notice any substantive transformation. At the same time, I knew that I had made a very sincere effort. What I mean is, I felt that I had done my part as prescribed by my theology of growth. I put forth significant effort in my spiritual practices and in obedience to the Word, but the change I hoped for had not come. Walking to my car in the church parking lot one Sunday morning after service, I had another "episode of honesty." I finally admitted to God and to myself that my Christian life didn't work.

This confession took a lot of courage because I was consciously aware of the two possible implications of this pronouncement: either my understanding of the Christian life was wrong, or Christianity itself was ineffectual. And the latter implication had further implications of its own.

Unknown to me at that moment, a third possible implication was buried in my heart. Within days of my parking lot encounter with God, this possibility emerged in my conscious mind. I was leaving my house one sunny Saturday to go grocery shopping. As I walked to my car, I looked out across the neighbor's spacious field toward the barn I could see from my living room. And at that moment, the thought entered my mind, "What if my understanding of the Christian life is right, but God simply isn't meeting me the way He meets others? What if He doesn't love me as much as He loves them?"

Something about this question felt like a conclusion. I suddenly experienced myself as "less than" those who God loved more than He loved me. I was on some outer ring, orbiting those He held closer to Himself. And the distance felt "matter of fact"; it felt true. It also felt horribly sad and empty. What was I supposed to do with this conclusion and these feelings?

REPRESSION

Sadly, I wouldn't do anything at all about this development for a couple of years. I simply repressed it—sent it back wherever it came from. But, of course, it didn't go away. I still carried the conclusion with me wherever I went and it sometimes broke the surface of conscious thought. I just didn't know what to do with it, and it was too painful and disorienting to think about. I eventually learned that my belief in God's "favoritism" was not reality, and I discovered that my underlying theology of growth was also wrong. But these insights had not come yet. For now, I pushed everything down—the belief, the feelings of sadness and emptiness that came with it, all of it.

At the same time, I got more involved with Promise Keepers. I participated in stadium rallies in several states across the country—California, Florida, and Washington DC. What attracted me to PK was its *imperatives*—clear, simple, and compelling. For a time, these imperatives superseded the internal angst I felt over my lack of growth and its implications, and gave me a way to live that seemed to make sense. What I liked about PK—and still like—was that it:

1. Calls men to rise up and understand, embrace, and fully live into our biblical roles as men.

2. Concretizes this call into seven promises that are easy to understand.

3. Fosters community with other men to find the camaraderie, prayer, accountability, and encouragement we need to keep these promises.

I love this.

My father was deeply impacted by Promise Keepers, and he invited my uncle, brother, and me to join him for a stadium meeting in Jacksonville, Florida in the late 1990s. Over 50,000 men singing "How Great Thou Art"! It was like a window onto the world as it was meant to be—men humbly coming together from all walks of life to worship God and to learn how to be better husbands, fathers, church leaders, friends, bosses, employees, citizens. I could feel the part of my soul that longed for, and was made for, this type of connection with other men. When we were given the opportunity to gather in small clusters to share honestly with each other and to pray together, the four of us huddled up. There we each shared something in our hearts that was holding us back from being all we were meant to be. We were vulnerable—we were *with* each other! We prayed hard for one another, too. Our bond deepened dramatically and crystallized into something I still carry with me today.

Needless to say, I am fully supportive of the resurgence of Promise Keepers currently underway.

However, PK seemed to fall short for me in one particular, but crucial way. It didn't help me deal with my repressed material, the things in my heart that I had pushed down over the years, whether consciously or unconsciously. I was striving with other men to be a better man, and there was some good in this. But, I also carried things in my heart that held me back and could not be transformed through confession, intercessory prayer, effort, and accountability alone. Something more was needed. Not only was I dependent on God to become the man I wanted to be, I was also dependent on God to put off whatever was hindering me. Apparently, Ephesians 4:22 required more than I was giving to it:

> You were taught, with regard to your former way of life, to put off your old self, which is being corrupted by its deceitful desires. (NIV)

I soon found myself back where I was before Promise Keepers came along. I had made all the resolutions I could make, and I had tried hard to carry them out. Yet, I wasn't changing into a man whose character was like Jesus' character, who exhibited the fruit of the Spirit from the heart. Instead, I felt like whatever was in my heart was a ball and chain that persistently worked against any substantive forward movement. There was only so much I could do without being freed.

DEEP BACKGROUND

I wonder if you also feel like you carry some vague, but powerful force that holds you back from the kind of growth you want to see in your Christian life. Many men do. Most of these men silently struggle to understand why their development is stunted. They search for ideas, for things they can do to restore forward movement. But, finding no answers or ideas, they are left only with uncomfortable realities. Their tendency—as was mine—is to push these realities deep into the background. They repress them.

Repression is a tremendously strong inhibitor in the Christian life. The "content" we push down sets itself up against any significant character growth and often demoralizes us. Moreover, what we suppress is more than just uncomfortable experiences in the spiritual life—it includes anything—past or present—that we don't want to face or accept.

Take a moment to study the figure below. I wasn't in my first seminary class very long before the professor, Dr. John Coe, slowly built a diagram of our hearts on the white board that ended up looking like this:[4]

4   From the course, "Introduction to Christian Spirituality and Prayer," Dr. John Coe, Talbot School of Theology, La Mirada, CA, September 2008.

This simple figure made me feel like I was looking in a mirror! Finally, somebody was talking about the way the heart really worked. The "Good" on the right, according to Coe, contains the parts of ourselves that we like and want others to see. These good parts can be qualities, gifts, talents, experiences, roles we play, etc. In general, we feel that showing these areas of our hearts secures for us the acceptance, respect, and love that we want and need from others. The "Bad" parts can be sin, dysfunction, immaturity, wounds, insecurity, failures, guilt, shame, sadness, anger, etc. We desperately keep these parts of ourselves hidden from others because we tend to feel that they compromise any acceptance, respect, or love that we might otherwise secure for ourselves. More than this, we don't feel that God wants these pockets of unsightly material either. And we have nothing to do with them ourselves because we don't know how to handle them and we want to believe that they aren't true about us! So, we push them down. We repress them.

Dr. Coe highlighted that there is nothing shocking about our repression. It is normal. In fact, Coe took us through Genesis 3 and demonstrated that hiding our bad and showing our good is exactly what Adam and Eve did with God immediately after they sinned. We inherit this unconscious tendency from the father and mother of the human race. The disposition to hide the bad and show the good is *hardwired* within us. It is what we all do! The only differences between us might be (1) the degree to which we repress unwanted truths about ourselves and (2) the specific things we try to keep out of sight.

We also maintain what Dr. Betsy Barber calls a layer of numbness that separates our conscious experience from the truth that we have repressed.[5] We keep our distance from the unwanted material through a variety of means, including busyness, distractions, roles and responsibilities we have, even our theology of growth. Whatever it takes. We not only want to avoid dealing with the content buried beneath the surface, we don't want to recognize that it's even there.

Not surprisingly, then, we bring all of our repressed material right into the Christian life. Yes, we are new creations in Christ (2 Corinthians 5:17). The old has gone and the new has come. According to Dr. Coe, this means that we are no longer alone at the very center of our lives. We have the Holy Spirit indwelling us. We also have a new love for God and new desires to please Him at the very core of our being (or our "inner being" as Paul says in Romans 7:22). These core desires become our conscious intentions—we want to be the kind of men God wants us to be and live the set-apart lives He calls us to live. But we struggle. We live much of life in Romans 7. Coe said that we don't intend to sin, therefore, but sin "leaks" out of us. We don't get up in the morning planning to blow up at our wives or our kids, for example, but something happens and BAM! Anger leaks out of us all over the place.

Coe's description of the heart made sense of Romans 7, as well as Ephesians 4:22. Our repressed material is part of the old man, the former manner of life that wages war against our new life in the Spirit and needs to be put off. But it doesn't go easily…our tendency is to "superficially" put off these parts of ourselves, according to Coe. We might try to ignore our anger altogether, for example, and believe that it's not there, or that it's not a real problem. We sometimes simply strive

5   From the course, "Intensive Journey Inward and Retreat," Dr. Betsy Barber, Talbot School of Theology, La Mirada, CA, February 2009.

towards love, patience, kindness, etc. and hope that our annoyance dissipates over time. Or we often pray quick prayers of repentance and ask God to take away our irritation and make us different. But these approaches are usually ineffective. Something more direct and dramatic is required to put off what we have pushed down.

For most of us, this hidden content becomes a ball and chain that we unwittingly allow to remain fastened to our ankle. The weight is too much for us, and the ball holds us firmly in place. I will talk much more about repression throughout the book—it is so important to face our hardwired tendency to push down unwanted truths about ourselves. I will also map out a way to identify the most significant things we have pressed down. Our goal will be to find God in these hidden things and His love, truth, and healing. We want masculine wholeness! But, for now, I encourage you to take the important step of talking openly with Him using the questions on the next page.

A NEW ADVENTURE

Not knowing in 1999 how to deal with my own ball and chain wouldn't be a problem for a while. A change in circumstances brought a significant and much-appreciated distraction: I was heading overseas! I had pursued the assignment in Kazakhstan as a last-ditch effort to stay in the Air Force and yet do something I felt passionate about. After a long application process, and a good grilling from a 10-person interview panel in DC, I was selected as the next US Air Attaché to the Republic of Kazakhstan.

I was taking a big risk career-wise. I gave up my slot at the Defense Systems Management College, and I declined the

Pentagon job offer. Senior leaders at the laboratory counseled me a couple of times that switching specialties from program management to foreign relations—especially Central Asian affairs—at this juncture in my career would likely mean stagnation. And they were right. But this was a wonderful opportunity and a great adventure. I reported to Washington, D.C. for training.

FOR PRAYER AND DISCUSSION

Consider these questions with God and, if possible, write down your reflections.

1. God, do I have things in my heart that trouble me? What are some of these things, Lord? Are there places of sin, wounds, dysfunction, immaturity, pain, anger, failure, guilt, shame?

2. What do I tend to do with these troubling places of my heart? Do I often repress them? Do I hide them from You and others, and even from myself?

3. If I talk with You about these things, Lord, what do our conversations usually look like? Am I often praying quick prayers asking You to change what I see?

4. How do I usually keep these hidden things out of my conscious mind, Lord? Do I use busyness? Distractions? Responsibilities? Theology? What, Lord?

NOTE: It is important to engage freely with these questions and others like them that will follow. If you feel you have scriptural/theological reasons not to look at your own heart this way, please read the appendix before continuing.

4

WARTIME DIPLOMACY AND DRY WELLS

O**N JUNE 1, 2000, I FOUND MYSELF ON A** Lufthansa flight heading for Central Asia. I remember only one thing about that flight—the emptiness of the land below. About four hours outside of Amsterdam, I woke up from a very brief nap—I am an awful sleeper on airplanes—and groggily gazed out the window into the night. There were very few clouds as I recall, so I had an unobstructed view of the Earth below. And I noticed something that rocked me: *nothing*!

Nothing was down there. Just land, endless land. Only once in a great while did I see some sign of people living below: a single, lonely light shining in deep blackness here, a very small cluster of isolated lights there. But, mostly, emptiness. A feeling like gravity swept over me, filled me, settled into my gut and my bones. And words instantly came with it: "You dumbass! What have you done? What were you thinking?"

I spent the next hour or so mocking my naïveté of the past year. I never anticipated this moment? How could this be? There is nothing like a violent experience of reality to bring perspective.

I had been caught up in the rush of it all. Selection to a competitive, challenging, and exotic post was a huge boost for my ego. Then the move to DC and all the busyness it brought with attaché training, language training, and meetings and briefings with every government agency you can think of. During the year I spent in Washington, I didn't have much time and energy to look past my current reality. Training was intense, and language training in particular was draining: one-on-one with a native Russian speaker five hours a day, plus loads of grammar and vocabulary homework. Fear drove me on—that familiar fear of failure. And when driven by fear, all of my energy goes toward mitigating that haunting and gnawing emotion. I kept my head down.

When we landed in Almaty, Kazakhstan, the city was deep asleep. U.S. Embassy personnel met me, helped me through Customs, and drove me 30 minutes or so to my new home. The streets were dark and a benevolent fog masked my view. What I was able to see looked strange to me, but not in the comprehensive sense. The architecture of most of the buildings was different—boxier—than I was used to. But that was all I noticed. Maybe my 27-hour journey had brought me to another country after all and not to another planet.

Not so. I woke up the next morning in a very large and luxurious home, and for a moment felt something like hope. But this flicker of feeling was snuffed out by the reality I now faced. My spirit of adventure—something I'm happy to possess—was completely overwhelmed by an earth-shaking and unmitigated uncomfortable-ness that would abide for the next several weeks. As I left home to meet my driver, Almaty slammed into me.

Everything was different—looked different, sounded different, felt different, even smelled different! Soon I would know that everything tasted different, too. "Comprehensive" is the only way to capture how "other" things seemed to me. It's interesting to remember the things that bombed my senses that first morning in my new home. Strange-looking trees dropped pungent pods on the ground and on the steps that led from my door to the parking lot. Little, boxy cars emitted puffs of smoke that didn't smell like smoke, but choked me just the same. Electric cable cars sparked and snapped as they rushed by and blasted me with wind. Old ladies in dark dresses swept the sidewalks with brooms made of straw. And the mountains…the mountains loomed large over the south side of the city and made everything feel small and nestled together. I was in the pages of a storybook.

I also had much to do, and I dove into my duties from the first hours of my first day. One of my primary duties was to manage the massive engagement program we had between U.S. Armed Forces and the Kazakhstani Ministry of Defense. The program included some 30 activities per year, ranging from information exchanges to joint antiterrorism exercises involving hundreds of troops. And God seemed to bless my orchestration of these activities. He gave me success and favor with both Kazakhstani officials and with my new colleagues in the Embassy. And behind the bustle of work, God did something for me that dramatically changed the course of my next two years.

I was sitting at home one Sunday afternoon contemplating my all-inclusive angst when God invaded my thoughts. I immediately realized that I had developed a coping strategy to ease my distress: *I kept reminding myself that it was temporary.*

I would be gone in a relatively brief amount of time. I was getting through the uncomfortable "present" moments by focusing on leaving in the near future.

This approach was my idea—unconscious or conscious—and God seemed to have something different in mind. He wanted me to embrace reality. He wanted me to let go of my old life and *live* in Almaty—make it my home, and not look past it. With His help, I was able to see the goodness and wisdom in His prodding and begin to live into it. My experience changed almost immediately. It wasn't long before the City of Apples and its people became very dear to me.

THE TOWERS FALL

My first year in the Capital was characterized by many of the things that described my experience before moving overseas. I worked hard, established myself in the only English-speaking church in the city, stepped out in ministry (I facilitated the Alpha Course in my home), and made new friends. In my personal relationship with God, I was also doing what I had always done, and it seemed to be working. I maintained a sturdy devotional life—morning Scripture reading and prayer—and this rhythm kept at bay those disturbing thoughts from Ohio about lack of character change and all that it might mean. I was settling in. Even some of the cultural and language frustrations that emerged early in my tour were resolving themselves for the time being.

Then the war came.

When the towers fell on 9/11, I was with my girlfriend in her home having dinner. I got a call telling me to come to the Defense Attaché's house, and it was there that I learned what had happened. A group of us watched the video of the planes plunging into the World Trade Center over and over again. And we struggled together to wrap our minds around what we saw—to somehow understand that this horrific tragedy was real—and to consider what it might mean.

Within weeks of the attack, the United States launched Operation Enduring Freedom (OEF) in Afghanistan. The war had started. Kazakhstan was a slowly emerging ally in those days. We had nuclear non-proliferation agreements with the Kazakhstanis and appreciated the country's strategic location, relative stability, tentative western leanings, and massive oil reserves in the Caspian Sea. But it still remained somewhat in the backwater of international life.

This was about to change. Kazakhstan's proximity to Afghanistan and our growing US presence in neighboring Uzbekistan and Kyrgyzstan brought the Kazakhstanis into the conversation about potential bases in the area. But, more importantly, the huge land mass occupied by this former Soviet Republic—it is the ninth largest country in the world—was directly on the shortest flight path between Afghanistan and US bases in Germany, where fresh troops and supplies were marshalled and hospitals treated our most seriously wounded warriors. We needed unrestricted overflight rights, and we needed emergency landing options for our aircrews.

And so began the most stressful period of my life. Since I was the US Air Attaché, the Ambassador sanctioned me to conduct negotiations with the host nation. I shuffled incessantly and at all hours of the day and night between Almaty in the south of Kazakhstan and the "northern capital," Astana (now known as Nur-Sultan), on the frozen steppe skirting southern Siberia, 600 miles away. By day, I led negotiations and documented the agreements we reached and the issues to overcome. By night, I coordinated with our Departments of State and Defense through the Ambassador and dialogued with the Air Force operational commands that would utilize whatever rights we were able to secure. At all times, I felt intense pressure.

I am still very thankful for the support staff that did so much to make me as comfortable as possible during this extraordinary time. When I had to rush from Almaty to Astana for meetings, all I had to do was call my executive assistant and interpreter, Anna. She would arrange my meetings with the Ministries of Foreign Affairs and Defense, make airline and hotel reservations, alert our driver, and even call my housekeeper to have her lay out clothes for me to quickly pack. We would usually meet with Kazakhstani officials shortly after landing in Astana in a large conference room with Anna and me on one side of a massive table, and more than half a dozen host nation representatives on the other. There we would press as far as we could go for the day, then coordinate with our respective stakeholders late into the night and, usually, into the early hours of the next morning. Then, after grabbing whatever sleep could be found, we would reconvene the group and dive back into our talks.

By God's grace, negotiations moved quickly and proved successful. I was surprised by the very few sticking points we encountered in our talks. Kazakhstan borders both Russia and China, and I knew that while I was coordinating with US stakeholders at night, the Kazakhstanis were doing their part to garner all the benefits of helping the United States without upsetting their superpower neighbors. Whatever they did or said worked. The United States and Kazakhstan signed bilateral agreements allowing our aircraft—and eventually, all

Coalition aircraft—to fly over its territory and execute emergency landings if necessary. As of today, many thousands of planes have safely flown the route we designed together.

I was excited—and more relieved than words can express—to have the negotiations behind us. But there would be many other heart-stopping emergencies to fill the space vacated by the completed talks. One in particular stands out to me because it was so unique. I didn't know this, but nations throughout the world have a formal mechanism for recognizing the legitimacy and sovereignty of other nations. So, when there is a regime change somewhere in the world, other sovereign states decide whether or not to recognize the new government and establish diplomatic relations. Well, we had just changed the regime in Afghanistan.

So I get a call one day from the Ministry of Defense's Chief of Foreign Relations asking me how Kazakhstan might send a delegation to Kabul. Of course, the honest answer was, "I have no earthly idea. And do you know there's a war raging down there?" But I somehow managed to collect myself and squeak out something like, "I'm on it."

What my promise really meant was that I would make some calls. Central Command—CENTCOM—was the Combatant Command responsible for all operations in the region, so I got in touch with an officer on their operations planning staff. To my surprise, he didn't seem surprised! This was, needless to say, a great relief and a source of genuine hope. I told him what I needed and gave him the dates and times the delegation would like to travel. He did all the rest. In a matter of hours, I had a route and call signs for the Kazakhstani aircraft. I put all of this information in a Diplomatic Note, affixed the Seal of the United States, and took it directly to the Ministry of Foreign Affairs.

It would be a few days before I heard from anybody in the host nation government. In the meantime, I ruminated on the process I had followed to secure the information needed to get the Kazakhstani aircraft safely in and out of Kabul. I couldn't help but feel anxious for the safety of those who would travel the route I had instructed them to take. My gut twisted and sometimes ached. I felt heavy and depressed. But I finally decided that the only thing I could do was trust my contact in CENTCOM and do what he said. This turned out to be a marker moment in my career. I finally learned—in my gut—the absolute need to trust my fellow servicemen and servicewomen.

Then the phone rang. A high-ranking general officer summoned me to Kazakhstani Ministry of Defense (MOD) Headquarters. I gathered my driver and interpreter and immediately left the Embassy. We arrived at the gate to our destination and realized that we had no idea what to do next. The place was massive—and gray, of course—and heavily guarded. Whenever I had been there before, our escorts were waiting and didn't allow us to mill about. We saw no one who didn't have a gun. Then, before we could look at each other and ask the question on all of our minds, the door opens and the general slips into the seat beside me!

Thus began our meeting. I can only speculate why he wanted to meet in our car and not in his office. But the irregular rendezvous did provide some assurance that the car wasn't bugged as we assumed it had to be.

The general wasted no time. I don't even remember introductions—since I had not met with him before, I just assumed we would start there. Instead, he gravely locked his eyes onto mine and asked a single, simple question: "Can you guarantee me that our delegation will return safely from Afghanistan?"

Uh, no.

Of course, I didn't actually say this. But I took a moment to consider the possibility of a lone foreign aircraft darting in and out of ongoing combat operations in a war zone. What level of guarantee is objective and appropriate? But, again, God was kind to me. My earlier ruminations had prepared me for this question. So, I returned his intense gaze, and told him with authority: "If your crew flies exactly as instructed in the Diplomatic Note, they will be safe."

This assurance seemed to be all that he needed. He was gone as quickly as he came. And the day of the diplomatic mission soon arrived. The MOD informed me when the delegation launched. They were scheduled to return in three days.

I learned early in my career how to maintain an air of calmness when my insides were freaking out. I almost always got away with it publicly. In private, there were prices to pay. I think I had diarrhea for all three days. And there were moments when thoughts of the worst tormented me. I didn't even know if they arrived safely in Kabul! I was left to fill the information void with my fears, which I almost always do.

After three interminable days, the delegation touched down safely in Almaty. With nobody from the host nation on hand to see me constantly running to the bathroom, I gained the status of something like a hero. I could make anything happen and instill confidence in all around me. I even received a very thoughtful gift from the MOD. I said nothing to recalibrate this perception, of course. Leverage is a wonderful thing.

MY DEFENSES FALL

Dozens of these emergencies popped up to "supplement" my ongoing responsibilities for ensuring smooth transit of troops and supplies for OEF, as well as other sensitive duties. But, behind the scenes of this work and pressure, another story—a much deeper story—was starting to unfold. It seems that the intensity of work, the never-ending adjustment to another country and language, and my beautiful girlfriend whose highest values were connection and truth-telling, all converged to form a tsunami that crashed through my defenses and left me disoriented and scared.

I began to admit—among other things—that my spiritual life was coming apart. By this time, I had noticed a lack of deep character transformation for years. When I noticed this lack of change in LA, I resolved to try harder. In Ohio, I repressed this awareness and all of its implications and stoically moved on. Now, something new happened: the well went dry. What I mean is, Scripture reading was dry and boring. Prayer was duty. Church a discipline. Sermons repetitive and tedious. I remember looking at my chair one morning—the chair I always sat in to read and to pray—and allowing myself to think this thought without quickly subduing it: "Oh, Lord, I don't want to do this anymore."

This confession terrified me. And my fear turned out to be a huge obstacle to progress of any kind. I was too afraid *not to* read and pray. And, saddest of all, I didn't feel I could talk more with God about my true feelings because they completely unnerved me. I didn't believe Christians were supposed to be bored by God's Word and prayer, or lament on a Sunday morning at the prospect of going to church. The Christian life isn't supposed to feel heavy and burdensome, is it?

So, again I pressed on—I continued to slog through. I read and prayed and did all the other things I thought I should do. But, one thing had changed: I now knew *why* I was pressing on. There were four main reasons that I was consciously aware of:

1. I was afraid that my experience of dryness meant something was wrong with me. However, I would have to face this possibility only if I actually stopped doing my spiritual exercises. If I did manage to continue on, then I must be okay, right? Maybe this was the way the spiritual life worked—you press on when you don't want to and this proves your genuineness and disproves your apathy. Or, in other words, perseverance demonstrates that the feelings of boredom and frustration aren't true about you. They don't ultimately characterize the "deeper, truer, essential you." I hoped so.

2. I didn't want to feel guilty for not doing what I felt I should be doing. Hunkering down and "gittin' 'er done" is better than feeling guilty all day. So, I actually used my spiritual practices to manage my emotions and feel better about myself.

3. I didn't know how God would react if I dropped Scripture reading and prayer in particular. I guess I saw my relationship with God as somewhat causal: if I do what I'm supposed to do, He will bless me. And the prospect of losing His blessing in the middle of a war terrified me!

4. I didn't want to change what I was doing because so much of my identity came from my devotion to the Lord. I felt good about myself in my consistency and when others reflected back to me their respect or even

admiration. I felt like I was seen as an example to follow. I didn't want to lose this esteem.

With so much riding on my perseverance, I resolved to persevere.

But my resolution was no match for reality. I had seen too much, admitted too much. I could no longer push down my emotions and choose to believe that all was well. Cracks and fissures formed and grew in my compromised layer of veneer, and repressed material started leaking out.

Walking home after work one Saturday, I was completely rocked by sudden and unbidden glimpses of my inner darkness and instability. All that was going on in my world, and all that I had begun to understand about my devotional life, broke open enough space in my facade to allow things inside me to erupt into consciousness. I saw flashes of the truth of my heart deep beneath the surface. There was sin, insecurity, disconnectedness, emptiness, loneliness, and sadness. I felt like I was abruptly meeting parts of myself that I was almost entirely unaware of. I was thrown completely off balance—I thought these powerful emotions might engulf me. I felt the impulse to run. The eruption so unhinged me that I went immediately to a nearby store so I could interact with people. I needed to take the edge off of the eruption and bring my mind back to the surface of my life.

It worked. I wasn't overwhelmed, but I felt deeply shaken.

And I felt scared to go home. What if this happened again? What if I couldn't control it next time? Fortunately, I was able to cap the spewing cavity by watching a tape of the Orange Bowl game my buddy Mark sent me. Distraction worked: I was okay for the time being.

FACING DRYNESS

What about you? Is your spiritual life dry, boring, and burdensome? Are you afraid something is wrong with you or that God has stepped back from you? Again, you are not alone! Turns out that dryness is a common experience that most of us face at some point in our journeys with Jesus. So, we need to further explore this "desert" experience. We will unpack it in more detail in the next chapter, including causes and appropriate responses. But, for the time being, please consider two exhortations:

1. Your experience of dryness might not be something you have caused, but something God has initiated!
2. Honesty remains our meta-virtue. Share your experience with God as openly as you can. The "Prayer and Discussion" section will help you do this.

I realize that it will likely be difficult at first to share your dryness with God. After all, you don't know what it means yet. Why is it there? What are the implications? Unknowns are fearful things. However, at this stage of our journey together, we just want to be in reality with God. If you feel dry, you are dry. Simply accepting this fact is the place to start.

WRAPPING UP

I was okay for the rest of my tour in Kazakhstan; there were no more eruptions during the last few months I was there. When it came time to consider next steps after Almaty, I had some offers. I could serve as the Air Attaché in Uzbekistan. I could also serve on the CENTCOM staff or teach at the Joint Military Attaché School. But, one of the benefits of hardship tours, like the one I had in Kazakhstan, is that you get to choose where you go next. I chose Los Angeles.

My time overseas had been a spiritual and emotional wake-up call. Looking back, I think that God had to take me well outside of my comfort zone to reveal things about my heart that He wanted to address. How far He took me is telling—I was deeply committed to not seeing these upcoming projects of His. It took a lot to open my eyes. Los Angeles offered a familiar place where I could make a solid contribution to national defense while getting the help I needed. And some lifelong friends would surround me. It was a no-brainer. So, on June 1, 2002, I took off from Almaty in the middle of the night.

Leaving Kazakhstan was surreal. I couldn't believe that— in an instant—everything I had carried on my shoulders was gone. And my new friends and my colleagues were gone. I was swimming a bit; I didn't know how to feel. The airplane was dark and quiet and reflected my mood.

After brief stops to visit friends in Egypt and to attend my high school 20th reunion in Florida, I landed in the City of Angels. Here I would come to learn that I had entered a season in my spiritual life called the Dark Night of the Soul. And here I would understand that my emotional experience came from a place deep within called the Cauldron or the Hidden Heart. But I'm getting ahead of myself. First, I would experience something called reverse culture shock.

FOR PRAYER AND DISCUSSION

Consider these questions with God and, if possible, write down your reflections.

1. Do I feel like the well is dry, Lord? Is Scripture reading and prayer boring and burdensome?

2. IF YES: What has been my response in this time of dryness? Have I pressed on with my reading and prayer and muscled through? Have I rushed through these spiritual exercises superficially? Have I abandoned them altogether?

   a. How do I feel in this season? Am I confused? Scared? Do I feel guilty?

   b. What have my conversations with God looked like during this season? What have we talked about?

3. IF NO: What do I think about the possibility of my spiritual exercises becoming dry, boring, and burdensome?

   a. How do I feel when others share about their experience of dryness in Scripture reading and prayer, for example? Am I anxious? Comfortable? Can I give them space to experience what they are going through without trying to "fix" them?

5

LEADERSHIP AND DARK NIGHTS

THINK I KNOW WHAT IT'S LIKE TO BE IN TWO
places at once—which, in my opinion, isn't a great way to
live. Because I had so little time to prepare to leave Almaty,
I felt like I had been abruptly uprooted from my home there
and firmly planted in LA. And only a handful of days separated these two forceful actions. Emotionally, I had a difficult
time staying in sync with physical reality. Part of me was in
Los Angeles and glad to be here. Part of me was still at the
Embassy with that tight, high-powered team we had formed
and my close, supportive friends. It would be months before I
stopped looking at my email every morning hoping they still
needed me and wanting to feel the rush of urgent, critical work.

At first, they did need me. My former boss or my re-
placement would ask a question or two, or maybe want my
perspective on something. But they had to move on at some
point, and I had to move on, too. After almost 20 years, I can
still feel the loss.

The Oxford Dictionary defines culture shock as "the
feeling of disorientation experienced by someone who is
suddenly subjected to an unfamiliar culture, way of life, or set

of attitudes." I was prepared for culture shock when I moved overseas, although I didn't appreciate the magnitude of the "disorientation" I would feel or how it would spawn other strong emotions like frustration and anger. But nobody spoke a word to me about reverse culture shock when I headed back home. It can be embarrassing!

Within a week or so of arriving in LA, my friends took me to a Christian concert in Orange County. We arrived a good half-hour before the show and started to make our way through the massive parking lot towards the venue. Then it happened…without any warning whatsoever, my stomach turned sour, my chest tightened up, and tears streamed down my face. I still remember every detail—exactly where I was, exactly what I saw. My first priority, of course, was to regain my composure before my friends saw me weeping like a small child. Due to the everlasting grace of God, I was a step behind them and had just enough time to climb on top of those inconvenient emotions and stamp them down before they made me look ridiculous. My second priority was to get a sense of what in the world was going on.

It was the cars. There were luxury cars everywhere. And wherever there wasn't a luxury car, there was a very nice car—either brand new or, at least, clean and shiny. The affluence caused this eruption in me! Having been immersed in a developing country with close friends who were just getting by, I was unfamiliar with Christians possessing and parading such lavish wealth. The scene struck me forcefully and left me staggering. It would take months to regain my balance. And I have to say, the balance I finally found is a tenuous one. I am still knocked off-center by the wealth I see around me.

POOREST OF THE POOR

My new job at Los Angeles Air Force Base was challenging, but it didn't consume my weekends. So, I found an outlet for my growing desire to know and serve the poor, and that outlet would become a mainstay in my life for the next 11 years: a Christian community among the homeless near the Port of Los Angeles. Years before, a friend of mine started something called the Wilmington Bible Study (WBS). On the surface, this study offered two things to the homeless in this port city: breakfast and time in the Word. On a deeper level, WBS offered dignity and a place to belong.

The rescue missions in the area required needy men and women to sit through a church service before being fed. My friend Karen, along with her close friend Lindsay, wanted to send a different message to the homeless: "Your physical and emotional needs matter to God. First, we will eat and fellowship together, then we will study Scripture if you want to stay. Feel free to join us for our little church service or move on into the rest of your day." In essence, we treated these men and women as equals, which in reality they are.

This approach nurtured a growing sense of dignity and community among the homeless. And I loved it. We met every Saturday morning in a spacious park under a huge, sprawling tree only a couple of blocks from the port. 8:30 a.m. was coffee time—we brought lots of coffee and just hung out and caught up with each other for half an hour or so. Then we had breakfast together, large individual meals brought in from a local restaurant and served in warm Styrofoam containers. After breakfast we formed a circle with some folding chairs and began our study. Rain or shine, we were there. The roof of a large municipal building nearby had an overhang that jutted out so far that it formed something like a porch. If the weather was bad, we nestled under that eave.

Over time, the ministry grew. We fed about 70 men and women every week. The study remained intimate, though—probably around one dozen. And honest. I was both challenged and refreshed by brothers and sisters who openly shared their thoughts and questions about the passages we studied. They brought it all—extreme poverty, alcohol and drug addiction, mental illness, prostitution, demonic oppression, crime of every degree, abuse, and longing—stirred into a core, innate desire to know God and to be known by Him and others.

I don't want to romanticize what happened in the ministry. I crashed many times before I finally understood what we were doing and what ministry truly is. For the first three years, I stumbled and fumbled. I stopped a study because I became frustrated with people who constantly hijacked the conversation or showed no sign of genuine understanding or change. A prostitute threw her Bible on the ground and stormed off at my choice of words. I got sick at smells and the unfettered desire of one man to release wet, gurgling belches during breakfast. A member of our little congregation who had been a raging alcoholic for 40 years told me that I was completely naïve (I later learned that he was right). Spiritual darkness was all around, yet I knew next to nothing about it. The list goes on. But I found a mentor and close friend in the ministry leader, Ron, who was patient with me and offered me more and more opportunities to lead and to teach.

What I discovered dramatically changed my understanding of ministry and helped me open more to God in my own life: love.

God wanted me—called me—to love these souls. I was to receive these men and women without reservation, get to know and enjoy them, and serve them while placing no demands on their shoulders whatsoever. He would do what He intended to do. But the context would be love. This revelation set me free to just show up and depend on God. It simplified my life and my ministry. And it transformed my relationships with some of the homeless men—including the raging alcoholic—into genuine friendships.

I realize that I have mixed motives for talking about this ministry as a highlight of my second tour in Los Angeles. I include it, primarily, because my time with the homeless was so important to me as both a teacher and as a "mirror." As a teacher, service to the poor showed me that the fundamental disposition of God's heart toward us is love. At the same time, my life with these men and women mirrored my personal experience with God. As I was able to share more of my heart with Him and receive His forgiveness, acceptance, and love, I was able to extend acceptance and love to others in life-giving ways. Secondarily, however, I hope that there will be some men who read this and feel led by God to start something like WBS in their own cities and towns. Lord, may it be so.

SMOKE AND FIRE

Of course, my weekdays were filled with my primary mission in LA: to launch rockets. By the end of my tour, I was the Deputy Program Manager for the Delta IV rocket fleet. This was a great job—I got to be involved in all aspects of the program, from business operations and hardware manufacturing, to satellite integration and launch. But the job I think

I enjoyed the most was being Mission Manager for the first Delta IV Heavy launch.

The Delta IV Heavy is a hulk of a rocket—the largest ever flown for the Air Force. It stands 23 stories tall and weighs more than 500 midsized cars. And in 2004, it was unproven. It had never flown. Its mission, once operational, would be to deliver the nation's heaviest and most sensitive satellites into very high (geosynchronous) orbits. A geosynchronous orbit, or GSO, is high enough that the satellite does not orbit the Earth, it orbits *with* the Earth. It remains over the same patch of land at all times.

Since so much was riding on this new rocket, so to speak, the Air Force decided it would be best to fly a demonstration mission. The mission became known as Heavy Demo, and after being on base for about two years, I was named Mission Manager.

One of the most interesting things about government satellites and launch vehicles is that they are not insured. The government itself carries the weight of financial responsibility if a mission fails. So, in essence, the Mission Manager's job is to orchestrate all the work required to "ensure" that the rocket is ready to fly its mission with acceptable risk. To accomplish this task, there are two resources at the Mission Manager's disposal—something called a Launch Verification Matrix (LVM) and an army of Air Force, government, and contractor personnel with all sorts of engineering specializations to do the verification work.

There are other aspects to the job as well—including serving as primary interface with the payload "customer" and training the Day-of-Launch Team that sits in the Control Room and gives its "go/no-go" recommendation. But the bulk of the work is the LVM. Hundreds and hundreds of verification tasks must be completed and signed off on, from physical inspections of vehicle hardware and test history to complex analyses of trajectory design and fuel usage. Status briefings start out slow in the beginning of a mission cycle, but ramp up to weekly, then daily presentations as launch day approaches. It is an exciting job.

On top of the Heavy Demo rocket sat a "dummy" satellite that was designed to have many of the same structural characteristics as future payloads. With this collection of various hunks of metal, we could run computer simulations to make sure the rocket and satellite interacted well together. For example, we wanted to be sure that the launch vehicle would not induce loads or vibrations on future satellites that would break something. We intended to safely insert this dummy satellite into GSO and thus prove the readiness of the rocket for subsequent missions. We also decided to give a small, experimental satellite a ride to Low Earth Orbit (LEO) on the way. Everything was all set.

I remember two things about launch day at Cape Canaveral Air Force Station, Florida: Watching the booster take forever to get off the pad and clear the tower, then thinking, "That was quick!" when the liquid strap-on rockets shut down and were jettisoned from the core vehicle. Fortunately, the second event didn't immediately follow the first. But the strap-ons did shut down earlier than they were supposed to, and there were consequences.

The first consequence was that we didn't reach our targeted orbit. The first stage didn't burn long enough to do its part in getting us there. This anomaly would have to be corrected before we could fly again. The second consequence was that the experimental satellite saw LEO only from a distance. We tossed it in the Indian Ocean, where it rests today. I felt awful about this, of course, and sent my sincere apologies to the scientists who had worked so hard to design and build that satellite.

However, in the world of space flight we had what is known as a qualified success. We did demonstrate the flight-worthiness of the vehicle, which was our chief aim. Once we figured out what went wrong and corrected the anomaly, we would be ready to fly our first operational payload.

We discovered that the early strap-on shutdown was caused by something known as cavitation, which produced bubbles in the liquid propellant. When those bubbles uncovered a fuel sensor, the sensor told the flight computer, "All done!" and the computer obediently shut down and jettisoned the massive boosters. This problem was corrected and has never occurred again.

HONESTY, NOT REPRESSION

Here again, though, a lot was going on behind the smoke, fire, and roar of rocket launches. For the first time in my life, *I stopped spending so much energy trying to repress my distressing feelings, sin, wounds, and immaturity.* Instead, I did my best to allow my emotions and other truths to surface and breathe a little. And every week I shared these feelings and truths with my Christian therapist as openly as I could.

The eruption that Saturday afternoon in Kazakhstan had terrified me. The things I saw beneath the surface of my heart—the sin, insecurity, disconnectedness, emptiness, loneliness, and sadness—almost unhinged me. What therapy provided was a place where I could begin to look at this repressed "material" with somebody who could understand it, help me safely talk about it, and direct me toward God and transformation.

Time with my therapist was like honesty practice. I had repressed so much for so long that I didn't know how to simply feel my feelings. And I was unfamiliar with how I might articulate these emotions, explore where they were coming from, and understand what they might mean. Our weekly meetings made me feel safe and gave me solid traction in regularly allowing repressed content to surface. Soon I was able to begin sharing these truths and emotions with God on my own.

I doubt if it's possible to overstate how important this time was for me. I intentionally embarked on a deeper journey with God that would take me to unimaginable places and require more strength and courage than I knew I had. I was on a new trajectory now, but my destination was completely obscured. All I knew was that I had to press into the reality of my emotional and spiritual life with God and trust that I would find love and real change.

I would do most of my "pressing in" during the early morning hours. I like to be awake when the world is asleep and all is still and quiet. I made a habit of getting up at 5 a.m. for most of my career. I would make some coffee and sit in my favorite chair in the corner of my bedroom. A floor lamp cast a dim yellow light that illumined a small island around me. And there I would try to read my Bible and try to be honest with God about not wanting to read my Bible. The water was completely gone now. Scripture reading—and prayer, too—were dry as dust.

After some number of weeks or months, I found myself just sitting there in the mornings doing nothing. I didn't try to read or to pray out loud the way I used to. I still intended to be with God. It was still supposed to be our time together. But I didn't feel Him there the way I used to. It seemed that I was sitting alone, but I was also—somehow—becoming more comfortable sitting alone.

In these times of solitude and silence, I began to write. I don't know why I started to write. Maybe sitting alone with no distractions made me more aware of all the thoughts and feelings swirling around inside, and I figured I might feel less cluttered and scattered if I wrote them down. My goal was simply to unload, to unburden myself. If God wasn't in the room, I would write to Him.

Everything I thought and felt—at least the big stuff—found its way onto the pages of several thick journals. I wrote every day until I had nothing left to write about. I would even write about things—admit things—that were scary for me. For example, what if I had done something to cause God to pull away from me? Why was I angry? What made me feel hopeless and sad? Why was I afraid all the time? Why was I so insecure? Why did I seem to care so little about the spiritual things that used to give me energy? This went on for a couple of years. I had a sense that I was doing the right thing, and writing was a tremendous help in getting myself squared away before facing my days. So I just kept going.

Then, a marker moment. As I wrote in my journal one morning, I found myself aware that God was with me. The way I remember it, I was *intuitively* aware of His presence. I simply *knew* that He was there. It was gut-level knowledge of almost imperceptible presence. I was so relieved and excited by this realization that I turned all of my attention to Him at once! And He was gone.

At first I had no idea what had happened. Where did He go? More time would pass before I began to appreciate the significance of this event. Maybe until now, I had pursued God mostly with my mind. I tried to apprehend Him with my cognitive faculty and understand Him. And this pursuit was good—I had to start there. But God is infinitely bigger than what my mind can comprehend, and His thoughts and ways are high above me. Also, my understanding doesn't necessarily translate to experience. I can know, intellectually, that God loves me. But, do I experience His love for me? Can I say with Paul that I *know* this love that surpasses knowledge (Ephesians 3:19)? God somehow brought me to a deeper, more intuitive and experiential knowing through this season that I would later learn was a Dark Night of the Soul.

DARK NIGHT OF THE SOUL

In one of my first seminary classes, Dr. Todd Pickett taught us that there may be seasons in our lives when God seems distant from us.[6] In particular, Pickett said, we don't experience our spiritual practices the way we used to. Rather than finding pleasure in Scripture reading or prayer, for example, these activities feel dry and boring. Our minds wander. We seem to be alone, isolated from God. Instead of experiencing God with us, we experience the truth of our own hearts—our sin, dysfunction, wounds, immaturity, lack of desire for our devotional life, lack of love, fears, worries, etc. This experience of ourselves can be very unsettling and disorienting. Often, we feel guilty. We don't believe we are supposed to feel this way!

---

6 The course was "Developmental Spirituality and Contemplative Prayer," Institute for Spiritual Formation, Talbot School of Theology, La Mirada, CA, March 2009.

Dr. Pickett went on to explain that this change in our life with God concerns us, especially since there is no obvious reason for the difference. We are not sinning any differently than we used to, so it is unlikely that new or significantly greater sin has brought about this perceived distance from God. We are not depressed; other areas of life don't feel dry, boring, and lifeless. And we are not in the kind of trial that would overwhelm us and produce feelings of indifference, resignation, or apathy. So what's going on? What are we to do?

Seasons like this can be very difficult. We may feel certain that God has withdrawn from us, and we are left confused as we wonder what we may have done to cause Him to step back. Like the psalmist, we cry out:

How long, O Lord? Will you forget me forever? How long will you hide your face from me?

—Psalm 13: 1

When answers to heartfelt questions like these don't come, we are forlorn. But what if this perceived distance from God comes at His own initiative? What if He intends to use it to expand His home within us?

Over the centuries, according to Dr. John Coe, many careful observers of God's activity in the lives of believers have noticed something. When God feels we are ready, He may withdraw some of the pleasure we felt in our devotions and other spiritual exercises.[7] Since we associate this pleasure with God's presence, we conclude that God Himself has withdrawn

---

7 From the article, "Musings on the Dark Night of The Soul: Insights from St. John of The Cross on a Developmental Spirituality," John H. Coe, Rosemead School of Psychology, Biola University [Journal of Psychology and Theology, 2000, Vol 28, No. 4, 293-307].

from us. However, He is still with us. He will never leave us nor forsake us (Hebrews 13:5). This sense of withdrawal and aloneness we experience enables us to see deeper things in our hearts and spurs us to be more honest with God about them. In the vacuum of His perceived absence, God draws out the deeper parts of our hearts into relationship and connects us with our longing to have Him with us in them (Psalm 42:1-2).

Dr. Coe went on to caution us. Because our devotional life has become dry, difficult, lonely, and revealing, he said, we will likely face one of three temptations. First, we may be tempted to work extremely hard in our devotions to try to generate the pleasure we once had in them. Or, we may be tempted to go through our daily time with Jesus quickly and superficially. We might even be tempted to stop doing our devotions altogether. Coe encouraged us to embrace the difficulty, continue in all of the activities of our devotional life, and let these practices be what they are supposed to be for this season: revealing. In situations like these, we are to be as honest as we can about all that we experience. We bring everything to God—especially our brokenness—even if it feels as though He has left the room.

Pickett's and Coe's explanations of Dark Nights articulated my experience so well. What I had gone through finally made sense! And I was grateful to God for somehow guiding me to share all with Him, to write down everything I was seeing, thinking, and feeling in this season. Sharing with Him this way was exactly what I needed to do.

I wonder if you can relate to my experience of a Dark Night. When you have your quiet times, does God feel absent? Do Scripture reading and prayer feel dry, boring, and burdensome? Are you concerned that you may have done something to cause God to "step back" from you? Bless you if this is where you are right now. Dark Nights are truly disorienting experiences, and we don't know how long they will last. I do have three recommendations, however, that might help you navigate this time well:

1. Try to accept the purpose of a Dark Night. God is drawing you into deeper relationship. The things in your heart that you may have kept hidden will start to come out now in the vacuum of His perceived absence. You will experience more of the truth under the surface of your heart—your scattered thoughts, anxiety, fear, insecurity, lack of love, lack of desire for your spiritual practices, anger, sadness, immaturity, etc. Basically, you will not see God as much as you will see the truth of yourself.

2. Try to accept that God wants you to bring these truths to Him, even though you feel that He is distant or has left the room altogether. He wants to be *in relationship* with you in these areas of your heart. As I will discuss in the next chapter, it is "God with us" that heals and transforms us.

3. Try to be as honest as you can when sharing these places in your heart with God. Genuine relationship demands authenticity. I suggest you start by engaging with the questions in the "Prayer and Discussion" section coming up.

RETIREMENT

Within a year of emerging from my Dark Night, my 20-year Air Force career was coming to a close. I focused on finishing well. For me, this meant taking good care of the men and women who worked on the Delta IV—helping them understand and do their jobs, as well as writing their performance reports and setting them up for future success. The missions we flew were much more routine now. Every configuration of the rocket system was fully operational. It was a good time to move on.

When I told people that I had no immediate plans other than a sabbatical, they were happy for me and maybe a little jealous, too. How many people get to take lots of time off just to figure out what comes next for them? I bounced into my sabbatical, as usual, full of naïveté. My vision of rest, relaxation, and a steady stream of insights on the future was blown up pretty quickly. Sabbaticals can be hard work!

FOR PRAYER AND DISCUSSION

Consider these questions with God and, if possible, write down your reflections.

1. God, when have I talked with others or with You about things I have repressed? What was that experience like for me? What was the result?

2. How do I feel about sharing more of what I see in my heart with You, God? Have I not bought into the idea? Am I afraid? Anxious? Willing? Open? What makes me feel this way, Lord?

3. God, how did I react when I read about the Dark Night of the Soul? Was I dismissive? Confused? Was it a "YES!" moment?

4. If I feel I might be in a Dark Night, can I embrace the three recommendations on the previous page? Do I have reservations? If I do, what are they?

NOTE: Some people have genuine concerns about experiencing and sharing repressed parts of their hearts: *Is it navel gazing? Is it a distraction to ministry? Will I get lost in it?* These thoughtful concerns deserve thoughtful responses. I have included my reply in the appendix.

6

SABBATICAL AND FRESH VISION

GOD SAID THAT HE WOULD WORK ALL THINGS together to conform me to the image of His Son (Romans 8:28-29), but even a sabbatical? After all, I had a clear understanding of what this brief intermission would be about. I would take some time to decompress from 20 years of military service, then discern what God would have me do next. However, in the words of Donald Rumsfeld, there were "unknown unknowns." As it turned out, God had His own plans for my respite, and His program would require a lot of deep work on my heart.

With my uniforms blanketed neatly in plastic and hung in the far reaches of my closet, I began my sabbatical with three big questions: (1) what should I do with my days?; (2) what should I do with my life?; and (3) should I grow a beard? I didn't seem to mind at first that I had no answers to the first two questions. I opted for facial hair and asked God about the rest.

Silence.

No word, no impressions, no Scripture verses, no friends intervening with messages from on high—nothing. I reminded God that my two big questions were sincere, thinking that some authentic dependence ought to elicit a response. But, no. As the days and weeks went by, I became frustrated with God. Here I was offering my days and, well, the rest of my life to Him, and He didn't seem to have anything to say about it. There was no movement, and movement is a big part of what makes life feel meaningful for me.

This stillness went on for a solid six weeks. Then, as I was sitting in my chair in the living room one morning thinking about how ambivalent God seemed to be, I sensed that something had shifted. It was just an impression I had. God was not silent, even though He wasn't saying anything about what I should do or become. He seemed to be asking me the question I was asking Him! When I asked Him what I should do on any given day, I sensed that He responded with a question of His own: "What do you *want* to do today?" When I wondered what I should do with my life, He seemed to inquire, "What do you *want* to do with your life?"

Part of me was excited—movement! Part of me was surprised, however, because my honest answer to both of these questions was, "I don't know." But, hey, no worries—I'll spend my sabbatical days talking with a life coach about the rest of my life. He'll ask penetrating questions that draw forth from deep waters my true soul and all the desires therein. I will see my life's purpose, write it in a mission statement, hang it on the wall, and live by it for the rest of my days. It's wonderful to have a plan!

I hired the best life coach I could find, and he did ask very good questions. I was shocked and deeply frustrated, though, to find that I had no answers. It was as if I had no access to whatever part of me held the compelling desires he was looking for.

Life Coach: "If money were no object, and you felt no fear, what would you do?"

Me: "I don't know."

Life Coach: "At the end of your life, what would you most regret not doing?"

Me: "Not sure."

Life Coach: "What do you see in the world that feels intolerable to you? What *must* be changed?"

Me: "You asking me these questions?"

I felt somewhat hollow inside—vacant, vacuous. And my frustration grew. The casual "I don't know" that I naïvely started with was now transformed into something much more raw and existential: "Oh, God, *I don't know.*" I didn't know what I wanted to do with my life, and I wasn't sure how I would come to know myself well enough to find the answer. Calvin was right:

> Nearly all the wisdom which we possess, that is to say, true and sound wisdom, consists of two parts: the knowledge of God and of ourselves. But, while joined by many bonds, which one precedes and brings forth the other is not easy to discern.[8]

How well did I really know God? How well did I really know myself? I had no answers anymore. Only two things were clear to me. First, I needed to stop paying my life coach huge sums of money to make me feel depressed. I could pick up with him down the road when I discovered some inner material we could work with. Second, I would have to settle in for a longer sabbatical than I had imagined. As it turned out,

---

8   Institutes of The Christian Religion, John Calvin, Chapter 1 (I.1.i).

two years would pass before I confidently moved into the next season of my life.

After all, by the time we reach our forties, we're a significant mess. I'm not simply projecting my personal experience onto the masses here, but accepting a universal truth. There is good news, however: God is greater than our hearts, and His wisdom is unsearchable. There may be a thousand ways I am messed up—being generous—but God knows the handful of things that, if addressed, would make a tremendous difference in my life. Only in retrospect can I see how strategic He was. The way I understand it today, He addressed three principal things during my sabbatical: (1) my misconception of His intentions toward me; (2) a biblical theology of growth; and (3) some of my repressed material and my lack of authenticity.

GOD'S INTENTIONS TOWARD ME

I knew from years of good preaching and personal Bible study that God intends to conform me to the image of Jesus. But what did this really mean? I can't say that I had a conscious understanding of what conformity looked like. But I discovered that I did have an *unconscious* conclusion: that God would *empty me* until I was some kind of vacuous container—a "Joe suit"—for the Spirit. I would slowly disappear, and He would progressively "possess" me and live His life through me. No wonder I felt serious reservations about this journey with God. And no wonder I was both relieved and excited to find that I would not lose myself in the transformation process, but rather become myself.

I want to take a moment to unpack this statement because, on the surface, "becoming myself" may sound humanistic.

Romans 8:28-29 clearly tells us that God conforms us to the image of the Lord Jesus:

> And we know that for those who love God all things work together for good, for those who are called according to his purpose. For those whom he foreknew he also predestined to be conformed to the image of his Son, in order that he might be the firstborn among many brothers.

As these verses reveal, God is faithful to conform us, and He reinforces His faithfulness in the strong language Paul uses. Romans 8:28 implies that our conformity to the image of Christ is the "good" that God works toward in *all things*. Romans 8:29 says that we are *predestined* to be conformed to the image of Jesus. He will make this happen!

But, what does Christlikeness mean? If conformity to Jesus' image is our destiny, what does it actually look like? I avoided this question, along with Romans 8:29, for a long time. When I did read this verse—usually quickly and without much conscious thought—I was only slightly aware that I felt uncomfortable. But when I allowed myself the space and time to feel what was actually going on, I was surprised and unnerved to realize that I felt threatened. I heard sermons about transformation and winced; I sang worship songs about radical change with noticeable reservation. For example, when I sang lyrics asking God to make me "less" so He could become "more," I felt resistant, defiant. I couldn't make sense of it at the time, but I was angry!

I didn't believe that I could talk with God about these difficult feelings, though. I couldn't imagine that it was appropriate for Christians to feel resistant, defiant, and angry about

God's Word. How would God respond if I shared these feelings with Him? What did it mean that I had these emotions in the first place? The idea of firmly resisting the Word of God and whatever His intentions were was deeply unsettling for me. So I kept my feelings hidden from God and others, and often myself, as best I could.

Slowly I realized that I had stumbled onto another "Hebrews 4:12 moment." As I read Romans 8:29, the Word uncovered the truth of my heart: conformity to the image of Jesus made me angry. This revelation was not something God wanted me to repress, to hide. In the spirit of Psalm 139:23-24, He wanted to talk about it!

Once I finally talked with God about Romans 8:29 angering me, He helped me see what was going on inside. I didn't understand what transformation meant. I felt He didn't want me. He didn't truly love me—He just wanted me to become somebody else. He was trying to minimize me, set me aside, or make me disappear until only Jesus by His Spirit lived in me and I was no more. What about me? I didn't even know who I was yet. I was still trying to understand myself and become myself. If God did away with me before this happened, I would never have been! Annihilation was the deepest existential tension for me. And, of course, God knew.

Over time I understood and embraced the fact that God does the opposite of what I felt. He does not annihilate us; He makes us *ourselves*! He grows us to become the unique men He created us to be in Him. When we become more fully ourselves in Him, *reflecting the character of the Lord Jesus in our individual uniqueness*, God expands His rule and reign over the earth and diversifies the expression of His marvelous attributes. Imagine how much more vibrantly God would manifest His presence in the world if we were all becoming more loving and joyful, more at peace and patient, etc. in our own unique ways (Galatians 5:22-23). God's presence through us—millions of us—is a beautiful and powerful image of one of the ways He glorifies His Name. As one early church theologian said, "The glory of God is a human being fully alive."[9]

A (BRIEF) THEOLOGY OF GROWTH

The next thing God helped me understand on my sabbatical was how He grows us, how He makes us become these unique men and women who reflect the character of Jesus. My understanding would deepen significantly later on, but the beginnings of life-changing insight came during this time on the sidelines. Fortunately, I didn't ride the bench on my own. My friend Bryan walked closely with me during my respite. We were in similar places at that time; each of us was trying to figure out what the future might hold for us. However, Bryan brought something to the discernment process I didn't have: books! He was well read and had solid recommendations for me at appropriate times. He had a lot of wisdom from his own journey with Jesus, too. What a Godsend.

I devoured anything that presented a biblical view of growth that could supersede my old understanding. Life experience blew up my former model of Christian development. *Trying harder and harder to make myself a better man out of gratitude to Jesus was a futile and exhausting endeavor.* This philosophy was devoid of dependent relationship and openly contradicted John 15:5 and Galatians 3:1-3. I would learn much more about self-effort versus dependence in seminary.

---

9 Irenaeus was a second-century theologian.

For now, I was beginning to land in a healthier posture of relational need.

If I tried to capture what I now understand about the essence of growth, I would choose the phrase, "intimate togetherness with Jesus." And intimate togetherness is the language of *home*...Jesus uses surprising "home" language in John 14, for example. He employs the same Greek word (abiding) to describe the Father living in Him (verse 10) and the Holy Spirit living in us (verse 17). He then says something stunning in verse 23 (emphasis mine):

> If anyone loves me, he will keep my word, and my Father will love him, and *we will come to him and make our home with him.*

Verse 23 holds the promise that the Father and the Son, the living Word of God, have come to make Their home within us! This is something to marvel at and ponder: God is not only "out there" somewhere, but He is also living within us. However, He does not live His life within us somewhat separately from us. He does not merely "intersect" with our lives from time to time, revealing things to us, correcting and strengthening us. He is not exclusively focused on helping us see and do what is good. Yes, thankfully, He does these wonderful things for us. However, "making His home with us" is so much more: He *"does life"* with us in intimate togetherness. We were made for this.

I have my own sense of "home," but I have lived alone for many years. So I asked Bryan to describe for me what it is like to "make a home" and "be at home" with somebody. He is married and has two young children, and I value the warmth in their home. After some thought, here are the words he gave me to describe his experience:

Intimacy	Rest	Strength
Love	Restoration	Encouragement
Belonging	Rejuvenation	Knowing
Growth	Recovery	Being known
Communion	Family	
Communication	Transparency	

These words echo scriptural language for the home God is making with us.

Interestingly, Romans 8:29 not only reveals God's intention to conform us to the image of Jesus, it contains "home" language as well (emphasis mine):

> For those whom he foreknew he also predestined to be conformed to the image of his Son, *in order that he might be the firstborn among many brothers.*

God is using family language in this verse. And what happens in a family? If parenting goes reasonably well in our homes, siblings grow up in two fundamentally important ways. First, they share the same good character. Second, they are uniquely themselves. So, we want our children to have good character: we want them to be loving, kind, patient, etc. We also want them to become whoever God made them to be, and we discover and nurture their uniqueness as the years go by (consistent with Scripture, of course). We do not press them into some mold we impose upon them. The same is true in the family of God. He wants us to have the character of the

Lord Jesus in our individual uniqueness. He wants us to be more alive as the men and women He created us to be.

These three biblical perspectives, then, changed my life and became an integral part of my new understanding of Christian growth:

1. God is faithful to grow me, as much as possible in this life, into the man He had in His heart and mind when He created me. This means that my character will become more like Jesus' character (Romans 8:28), but I will flourish in my uniqueness rather than lose it. When I am more like Jesus, I am self-giving, not self-annihilating.

2. God transforms me through the intimate togetherness of home. I cannot grow at all apart from Him (John 15:5). As I abide in Him and come more and more under His influence (Ephesians 5:18), I become myself.

3. God works in all things to expand His home with me and "co-inhabit" more and more places of my heart with me (Romans 8:28).[10] At home with Him, I experience His presence, truth, forgiveness, acceptance, love, and companionship. God is about relationship and influence, not possession.

My early theology of growth dictated that I work diligently in the strength I have to conform my character to Jesus' character. And I trusted in a "secret" work of the Spirit to change me inside into a man who obeys from the heart and manifests the fruit of the Spirit. Now I see that the effort required in the

---

10 I use the word "co-inhabit" even though it is not found in the dictionary. The word means "cohabitate"; however, co-inhabit seems to convey a stronger sense of the reality of God's presence in our hearts.

Christian life is not directed at changing my character in my own strength. Rather, I put forth effort to *open my heart* to the One who changes my character *through His presence with me.* I invite Jesus to co-inhabit more and more places of my heart with me and work relationally with Him on character change. This way of growth is the slower, progressive, relational filling of the Spirit. And, interestingly, it seems to reflect something a friend of mine once learned in Sunday School when he was only a child. "Our hearts are houses with many rooms," so the teaching goes. God is with us in our house, but not necessarily in every room—we inevitably try to hide things from Him. We need to invite Him into these hidden spaces. Wherever we are alone, we need to be with Jesus.

REPRESSED MATERIAL AND FALSENESS

Armed with this new understanding of growth, I guess I was ready for my next adventure with God: deconstructing two major idols in my life. These two idols—self-image and people-pleasing—occupied large areas of my heart. God and I were not co-inhabiting these areas together. I was alone, and my idols were on the throne.

My idol of self-image took on two principal forms: physical appearance and personal importance. Both were born out of deeply repressed insecurity. And God went after each of them in the most practical ways.

For most of my military career, I was a gym rat. So were my friends. We enjoyed working out together and challenging each other. But I had become attached to my appearance as an athletic man. Especially since I had grown up skinny and was often teased, I was deeply invested in my new body and the respect I felt it won for me. However, I had become its slave.

Weight training in particular had grown old for me over the years. I didn't really want to lift any more, but at the same time, I couldn't stop. I dragged myself to the gym. Even when I was sick or hurt, I worked out. This workout "ethic" was entirely unhealthy. I can't say that I was surprised, then, when God impressed upon me that it would be good to set aside the weights for a season. I could still do cardio work to maintain my overall health, but weights would have to go.

What would I look like? What would others think of me? Who would I be without my powerful appearance and the respect it seemed to secure for me? I didn't know. This movement toward detachment from physical appearance was a simple act of obedience. It was a new "spiritual discipline."

I reluctantly pressed ahead. I disassembled my home gym, sold all of my weights, and prepared to ride out the storm of anxiety that was sure to come. It came. I found out how desperately I wanted to be distinguished from other men. Now, without a uniform and the body to go with it, I appeared to be losing ground to others. I felt like I was disappearing and they were becoming greater. My anxiety surged.

To take the edge off of my heightened anxiety, I unconsciously tried to prove that I was special by over-spiritualizing my sabbatical. When people asked me what I was doing, I had ready answers that made me feel important. I wasn't as busy as they were anymore, something that had brought me a sense of self-esteem for a long time. So I had to be doing something that they didn't have time to do and that was highly respectable: I was aggressively growing in prayer; I was working with a life coach to discern my call; I was possibly preparing for the mission field with a daring missions agency focused on unreached people groups. Ah, the trump card in Christian circles: missionary work! Certainly, people would respect me with the possibility of missions in the mix.

However, in the solitude and silence of my sabbatical, God helped me see what I was doing. The truth was that I wasn't very busy—I was using these answers I gave to inquisitive people to manipulate them and to relieve my anxiety. So God added another spiritual discipline to my abstinence from weight-lifting: an honest answer to these questions.

From this point on, when someone asked me what I was doing to fill up my time, I would say, "Not much. Just trying to discern what I want to do." "Not much" was hard to say at first. It seemed to mean that I wasn't important enough to have plenty to do. I felt less than others. And "trying to discern" made me feel weak, like I had to take so much longer than everybody else to have a sense of who I was and feel some confidence in what I felt called to do. However, I gritted my teeth and obeyed, and something wonderful started to happen.

My anxiety peaked in those moments when I told people that I wasn't doing much, but over time my baseline tension level dropped. I didn't seem to care as much about what others thought of me. My concern over the perceptions of others was still there and still strong, but not as strong. I was moving in the right direction. I was finding my true identity—that I belonged to God and that He loved me—rather than the elusive and fragile identity I once found in the reflection of others.

With God co-inhabiting my insecurity with me, I now had a stable home in a once chaotic, lonely, and fearful place in my heart. From this home, this "base of operations," we worked together towards less manipulative behavior and more authenticity, especially as He helped me through the excruciating process of redefining my codependent relationships.

I was beyond a mere people-pleaser. I was codependent. I would do my best to understand the needs and wants of others, then conform my own needs and wants to fit theirs. Somewhere deep inside, I believed that the more I was like others, the more I would be respected, accepted, and loved. I was a chameleon of sorts, changing colors to match my surroundings out of fear of the consequences of standing out. Of course, this way of living required one momentous sacrifice: repression of my own needs and wants.

Here's a law that stands up under scrutiny like the law of gravity: codependent people will find each other! If you put a hundred people in a room, and two of them are codependent, you will likely find these two talking together by the end of the evening. And so it was with me. Several of my friends were also codependent. At the same time, my enmeshed behavior was distributed throughout all of my relationships. God wanted more freedom for me, and He made His desire clear to me through my therapist and one of only two "God Dreams" I ever had. Now was the time to act!

The action God required was not complicated, but it was gut-wrenching. I would have to be more honest about my own desires in my relationships. He asked for honesty with love. I did my best to "show up" more in my family life and in my friendships. In one case, I barely found the courage to be honest—it was like I forced myself to do something that every part of me abhorred. Pushing through my resistance was like the first time I bungee-jumped—I made myself do what every part of me ran from. I wish I could say that all of my relationships deepened as I interacted with others more as myself, but there were terrible losses. While some of my bonds deepened and blossomed, others were destroyed. I had two friends, in particular, who severed their connections with me when they realized that they were not as central to my life as I had led them to believe. This loss was devastating. Years would pass before I could think of them without feeling pain. Fortunately, I also felt the benefits of living in reality with others. I was more consolidated as a person without my unchecked codependence; I was aware that I felt more "substance" to myself. There was a real person inside, not just an amorphous blob that took on the shapes of others. Simply put, I became more and more fully myself. My anxiety level dropped some, too, and tangible measures of inner peace and rest took its place. I even had a sense of what I wanted to do next—and I found it without the aid of my life coach! I wanted to be a spiritual director.

SAFE INVITATION

Knowledge changes things, doesn't it? I wonder if you have felt like I did. Maybe you, too, were reluctant to open your heart more deeply to God because you feared that He would either (1) "take over" and set you aside or (2) bury you under the impossible burden of dealing with whatever you found inside on your own. Or maybe you couldn't articulate your fear of greater intimacy with God or its source; you only knew that you felt threatened. Knowing His life-giving intentions toward us and the means He employs to fulfill them enable us to feel safe with God. Now we can invite Him to live with us in the most sensitive places of our hearts, even areas of deep insecurity. We just need to be brave. It takes a lot of courage to be weak!

FOR PRAYER AND DISCUSSION

Consider these questions with God and, if possible, write down your reflections.

1. God, what have I believed Your intentions are towards me? What did I think You wanted to do with me?

2. What does it mean to me to know that Your intention, God, is to make me more and more *myself*, the unique man You had in Your heart and mind when You created me?

3. God, what is my reaction to this three-point perspective of growth I just read about on page 120? How do I feel about Your desire to co-inhabit more and more places of my heart with me?

4. What about my repressed material, in particular? God, am I willing to invite You (at a reasonable pace!) into areas of my heart that I don't know how to handle, like ongoing struggles with sin, wounds, dysfunction, immaturity, pain, anger, failure, guilt, or shame? If not: what do You and I need to talk about, Lord, to get me to a more comfortable place with invitation?

NOTE: If you feel like you might be overwhelmed by inviting God into places of your heart that you don't know how to handle, I encourage you to return to this question after you finish the book. In particular, Chapter 8 and pages 161-162 of the appendix may be of special interest to you. Bless you.

7

SEMINARY, EXPLANATIONS, AND ERUPTIONS

BY THE TIME I REACHED MY EARLY 40S, I KNEW that I was done with school. I had already completed a couple of engineering degrees, not to mention all the courses and certifications required in military life, like Squadron Officer School and Air Command and Staff College. The thought of being in a classroom again made me wretch. So, I wasn't the first person to bring up the idea. My friend Sue was.

I didn't receive her vision with great appreciation. I felt hurt by it, actually. After being friends for many years, did she really know so little about me that she would encourage me to do the thing I most abhorred? And wasn't there another way to become a spiritual director? Couldn't I just be apprenticed to someone? Sue reminds me once in a while that she knew a lot more than I gave her credit for. So did a couple of other friends. Within a year of pushing back against them all, I was on my way to another round of grad school.

I had considered several vocational paths at the end of my sabbatical. The two years I spent on the sidelines helped me discover what I was good at and what was life-giving for myself and others. I noticed that I came alive when I was with others in the raw reality of their inner worlds, and I longed to help them find safe passage to greater health and wholeness. So, naturally, I considered becoming a therapist or a counselor of some kind. But the spiritual journey was central to my interests and passion. I didn't believe that Christian spirituality was an addendum to our lives. I wanted to know how Christianity *explained* our lives and all our experiences. And I wanted to know how our lives with God worked themselves out in the practical realities we faced—in our circumstances, as well as in our thought lives and emotions.

Spiritual direction training seemed to provide some of the answers. In direction sessions, we might talk about some of the same things that would interest a therapist, but we're not looking for solutions to these problems. We're looking for God in them. Basically, a spiritual director helps people discern for themselves where God is in the midst of their experience and what He might be doing. There is also the discernment of what cooperation with Him might look like. It is extremely rewarding work. And, as it turned out, Talbot was one of the best evangelical spiritual direction training programs in the country and only 45 minutes from my home! So, armed with benefits from my GI Bill, I jumped in.

What I learned and experienced there changed my life. I finally understood the cause and effects of repression, and I came into contact with some of my deepest suppressed material. At the same time, I gained a lot of traction in sharing these hidden areas with God and finding greater freedom and masculine "solidness." However, my initial experience of seminary was not at all what I had hoped for. In a word, it was an ambush. As I mentioned, I went to Talbot because I wanted formal spiritual direction training. What I got, though, was a much deeper understanding of the condition of my heart and my desperate need for the love and grace of God. Frankly, I was shocked.

WHAT WE ALL DO

The first thing that hit me about going back to school at the age of 44 was that I had become rather full of myself. Since Talbot School of Theology is part of Biola University, I was exposed to lots of young millennials who weren't wearing uniforms and didn't have to salute me. Whether I was in the bookstore, the coffee shop, or in class, I was now invisible or treated as an equal! I stopped by the IT Help Desk one afternoon to talk about a problem I had with my new email account, and the young man behind the counter burped up a stream of complex acronyms and technical specifications that meant absolutely nothing to me. I stared at him like a complete idiot, and in turn, he treated me like one! The impatience, the condescending tone, the incredulity at my lack of knowledge—I felt like handing him my resume or giving a speech. Who was this goober of a kid who dared to address me this way?

Spiritual director training? That would come later. First, humility training.

And that training commenced almost immediately. As I mentioned in Chapter 3, Dr. John Coe drew a figure on the whiteboard within days of starting my first class:

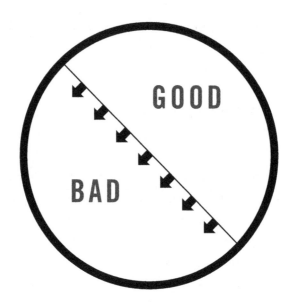

No effort at all was required to see myself in this diagram. Yes, I showed the world only what I wanted others to see. Of course, I hid everything else! I tried to live in the "good" part of my heart. I wanted to believe that the good was the real "me." Whatever felt unflattering, confusing, or too difficult to handle easily found its way into the deep background of my heart, where I hoped it would dissipate or disappear altogether.

But Dr. Coe didn't stop there. He helped us see where this way of life leads us, and his conclusion rocked me: *we build a life out of only remains.* We construct a whole persona out of only the good we choose to show and leave so much of ourselves behind. We also engage exclusively in things that will be congruent with the parts of ourselves we like and stay far away from activities and experiences that might expose something beneath the surface that we abhor. We are split men, trying to be good while carrying the weight of all that we've repressed. We are mere shadows of what we could be:

GOOD

In Coe's words, we become something like a caricature of ourselves. And his conclusion was well supported in the reading assigned for the class. Dr. Karen Horney (pronounced *Hor-nai*), in particular, points out that we go beyond our attempts to show only the good—we embellish the good![11] This embellishment is the crescent area enclosed by dotted lines in the figure above. I've certainly seen this dynamic in my own life. For example, I may be a good athlete, but I'd rather be known as elite. Or I may be intelligent, but I'd like to appear brilliant. *Dependable* becomes *absolutely unflappable*. You get the picture.

This way of life requires an enormous amount of vigilance and energy. I must constantly keep whatever I've repressed completely out of sight and project to the world the image of myself that I feel secures the acceptance, respect, and love that I crave. This projection is what Dr. Horney calls the idealized image of ourselves. Others call it the false self. This "self" is not

---

11   From her book, "Neurosis and Human Growth," W.W. Norton & Company, New York, 1950, Chapter 1.

completely true. At best, this portrayal of ourselves is only a shallow approximation of who we really are.

No wonder we feel like we're not bringing enough to our lives, that we're constantly reaching beyond ourselves. Leaving so much of ourselves behind and striving to become a version of ourselves we like leaves us feeling that we lack depth, substance, solid sturdiness, even manliness. Living this way is a primary reason why, I believe, a lot of us feel like guys and not men.

There is another possible outcome of repression as well: we may feel that we are men, yet we adopt a contorted view of masculinity that either conforms or reacts to our suppressed material. For example, a man struggling with repressed anger may adopt a "strong" view of manliness. He may value directness and firmness to such an extent that he becomes overbearing and, possibly, a bully. Another man may so detest his hidden anger that he adopts a weaker view of manliness. He may value kindness and gentleness to such an extent that he becomes passive. In each of these scenarios—whether we feel like guys and not men, or we feel that we are men yet have a distorted view of masculinity—we are not all that we are meant to be. Our repressed material is controlling our experience of life.

Dr. Betsy Barber also points out that the broken parts of ourselves we left behind hold the promise of more robust life for us. Not only is there sin, dysfunction, wounds, failures, immaturity, guilt, shame, sadness, anger, etc. in our repressed hearts, but there is also a much greater capacity for love, authenticity, joy, spontaneity, creativity, and many other life-giving experiences. For men, there is a fuller and more robust masculinity. These hidden parts of ourselves, then, need to be healed, not pushed down. The road to becoming more fully ourselves must take us into our brokenness.

LETTING GOD IN

This understanding of my heart made sense of all that God had been doing in my life over the previous 12 years. He was trying to bring the truth of my heart out into relationship with Him. The reason we go into our brokenness is that the healing we need comes relationally. It comes through *God with us* in the areas we've repressed in dark aloneness. God showed me in LA and in Ohio that I wasn't changing so that I would talk with Him about what I was really like inside. He withdrew the pleasure I experienced in my spiritual exercises in Almaty so I would recognize the thoughts, feelings, and inclinations of my deeper heart and invite Him to be with me in them. He compelled me to be more authentic during my sabbatical so He could be with me in the deep insecurities that fueled my falseness. He wanted to co-inhabit with me the very places I could not handle on my own or even admit were true about myself. *God wanted to love the "unlovable me" and raise me more fully to life as the man He created me to be.*[12]

Each time God called me forward, I felt threatened and either resisted or grudgingly moved ahead. Now in seminary, I finally saw what He was doing and embraced the honesty required to find deeper healing. And I was about to discover some things about myself that shocked me: fear, sadness, and anger.

---

12   The content of my repressed heart was not, objectively, unlovable. It only felt unlovable to me.

FEAR

I've wrestled with fear nearly all of my life. I thought, at some point, my fear would finally subside. After all, I had been so many places and done so many things. My expectation was that a track record would emerge, and the record would show that there was nothing to be afraid of. In fact, a storyline did become clear over time. My deepest fears did not materialize—everything seemed to work out reasonably well. And yet I still experienced a baseline anxiety level that was disproportionate to my circumstances. This apprehension clearly showed itself during my first silent retreat.

My seminary program required me to go on retreat every semester. The faculty designed these getaways to help students be with God without any distractions. They were *solitude and silence* retreats—no talking with others at the retreat center, no phone, computer, books, television, movies, music. Nothing to distract—only our Bible and a notebook. Since I was in California, several beautiful retreat houses were available to me. I chose one located in the spacious foothills of the San Gabriel mountains. It was a beautiful place, surrounded by tree-lined peaks with a river running swiftly through the property and coyotes howling in the distance. I loved it.

I settled into my small and plain cinder block room, had dinner, and headed out for a long walk. By the time I returned, I was tired and ready for bed. Being unplugged from all of the demands on me and surrounded by so much space and natural beauty, I felt like I could sleep for days.

So I was surprised and annoyed when I woke up at 12:30 a.m. and struggled to get back to sleep. I tossed and turned... by the time 1:00 a.m. rolled around, I was frustrated and angry—I was awake and there was nothing I could do about it.

But an idea popped into my head. I noticed that I was anxious and afraid, but I didn't know why. I thought that if I got up and took some time to write down whatever I might be feeling angst about, I would be able to jump back in bed and nod off. I sat in the only chair in the room, a primitive rocker, and started to write down the things that concerned me and made me feel jittery. As I started to write, a torrent of worries poured through my pen onto the page. Five things, 10, then 20, 24…by the time I sat back and tried to take stock of what happened, there were close to 30 items on my list and all of them had significant emotional content. I sunk in my chair.

I had tried for years to be less afraid. I knew the Scriptures that commanded me to trust God, and I applied them to my life as best I could. I prayed (Philippians 4:6), and I cast my cares on Jesus (1 Peter 5:7). I remembered how God clothed the lilies of the field (Luke 12:27-28) and gave good gifts to His children (Matthew 7:11). I also didn't let fear have the final say in what I would or wouldn't do. Yet here I was, sitting in the middle of nowhere, looking deep into my heart and finding it riddled with anxiety. Despair swept over me. I put down my pen and paper and just sat there. It was 2:30 in the morning, and I didn't know what to do any more.

Looking back, this is exactly where I needed to be: at the end of myself. I knew I had already tried as hard as I could to deal with my fear, so I wasn't tempted to double down on my effort. I needed Jesus. I needed Him with me in my anxiety to love me and guide me. I recognized—finally—that I was totally dependent on Him (John 15:5). Rather than try to rid myself of fear, I would ask Jesus to be with me in my fear. This invitation changed everything.

From then on, I was not alone in my fear, but together with God. We worked through my apprehension relationally.

"God," I would ask, "What am I afraid of? Where does this fear come from? Why doesn't my objective assessment of the situation change the way I feel about it? Why don't I trust You more? How do I grow in trust?"

God with me is what started to change my anxious experience of life. After all, perfect love casts out fear (1 John 4:18). I needed to experience more of God's love for me, and I couldn't lean into Him if I was alone in my fear. I had to invite Him in to co-inhabit this area of my heart with me. And I had to be open to whatever He showed me (Psalm 139:23-24) and to any resources He brought to help me, including some therapy.

SADNESS AND ANGER

Forty-eight-hour, solitude-and-silence retreats were not the capstone retreat experience in my seminary program, however. The *three-week* retreat was! I had heard about this retreat since entering the program in 2008. Now, in 2012, I was nearing the end of my course of study and my spiritual direction practicum. It was time for me to go.

In the longer retreat, all of the same rules apply as in the 48-hour retreats. I was to occupy a house in Gig Harbor, Washington, about an hour's drive south of Seattle. There, I would live for 21 days completely alone with no distractions whatsoever. In addition to the diversions forbidden during shorter retreats, I was not allowed to exercise. Working out, in any form, would dissipate my experience of suppressed memories and emotions and compromise the objective of the getaway. This purpose was simple and staggering: to weaken the layer of numbness that separated me from my repressed heart and to be with God in whatever emerged from the cauldron within!

To help me safely navigate the experience, I met every morning before sunup with a man named Bryan who was both a Christian psychologist and an evangelical spiritual director. Each day I drove the 10 minutes to his office in time to get there at 5:45 a.m. and present him with the journal that contained my notes from the previous 24 hours in isolation. After he carefully read through the notes, we began our session. After our meeting, I returned to the house, made breakfast, recorded anything significant from my time with Bryan, then took a shower. The rest of the day was completely unstructured until I wrote in my journal in the evening and went to bed. The only rhythms I tried to maintain were mealtimes and short (low-exertion) walks. Of course, I had stocked the house with food so that I didn't have to leave to buy groceries and risk interaction with other people.

I loved the house. It was massive and beautiful. The two-story home sat atop a long sloping hill, giving me a magnificent view of Puget Sound. I particularly enjoyed the bright and spacious great room, with its high ceilings, fireplace, and huge windows opening to a miles-long bay. On the second floor, an observation room allowed me to see all the way to the far side of the bay. Late in the evening, I would sit up there to watch the train that slowly passed on the south side of the water opposite the house. It was January—cold and rainy—and the lonely whistle barely reached my ears.

While the details of all that I experienced in Washington are deeply personal, I will say that my purpose in going on the retreat was fulfilled. God used the isolation to weaken my defenses and allow buried memories and emotions to surface into consciousness. And, oh my...what I experienced—in general—was a huge reservoir of pain and sadness, as well as shocking anger!

I took seven things away from that extraordinary time in Washington. These conclusions contributed significantly to my desire to write this book:

1. The dynamic of repression is categorically real.

2. We tend to push down whatever we don't want to see or experience about ourselves, whether it be some unsightly sin, painful memory, pocket of immaturity, or powerful emotion that we feel we can't handle.

3. Whatever we repress remains "pure." It does not go away, and it doesn't dissipate. It is as if it were frozen in time.

4. This suppressed content can occupy large parts of our hearts and control much of our experience of life. My lifelong depression, for example—as well as my melancholic temperament—is likely the result of repressed sadness and anger.

5. Hidden material often holds us back from becoming—as fully as possible—the men God created us to be. It is part of the hindrances mentioned in Hebrews 12:1 and the former manner of life in Ephesians 4:22.

6. God wants to co-inhabit these places of our hearts with us to bring healing, wholeness, and freedom to love (Revelation 3:20).

7. We don't have to go on a three-week retreat for this co-inhabitation to happen. As I will discuss in the next chapter, God will use life itself to show us the parts of our heart that we need to open to Him (Psalm 139:23-24).

GRADUATION AND BEYOND

Having completed the three-week retreat, I was ready to graduate. I managed to launch from seminary into the rest of my life, though, without a comprehensive ministry plan. I knew only one thing for sure: I wanted to continue to offer spiritual direction as I had done since beginning the direction practicum in 2010. The rest was unclear to me. However, opportunities eventually presented themselves. The next 10 years would ultimately involve many hundreds of hours of spiritual direction, as well as teaching and church leadership in a congregation of well over 2,000 members. What I learned validated my desire to add my voice to the conversation on Christian masculinity.

I found that we—especially in the conservative evangelical church—tend to focus on putting on the "new man." Simultaneously, we try to superficially put off the old man, including the content of our hearts that we have repressed. This approach to growth significantly stunts our progress toward genuine Christ-like character and fullness of masculine design. And it causes untold damage in church leadership as we come together to submit to Jesus as head of the body and jointly discern His will. Hidden parts of our hearts leak out, wounding others and compromising the discernment process. It breaks my heart. We need some directionality that enables us to deal more substantially with the brokenness we carry in our hidden hearts. In the next chapter, I try to outline a way forward that summarizes our journey in this book and provides my final thoughts on concrete steps for healing and growth.

FOR PRAYER AND DISCUSSION

Consider these questions with God and, if possible, write down your reflections.

1. Looking at the figure on page 133: God, what are the "remains" I have built a life out of? What are the good parts I choose to show? What are the embellishments?

2. Father, what do I feel the good parts that I show (and the embellishments) secure for me?

3. Do I feel like I lack depth and substance as a person? Do I order my life to avoid exposing myself as shallow or inadequate?

4. Lord, am I convinced that I need to be open to exploring my repressed material with You? Am I willing to invite You to show me what is there and ask You to co-inhabit these areas with me? What questions or concerns do I have?

8

CONCLUSION

I T'S BEEN YEARS SINCE I WATCHED THE MOVIE
Last of the Mohicans. The film has stayed with me, though.
It made a deep impression on me: the raw courage shown by
some, the admirable character of Hawkeye, a majestic music
score, beautiful scenery. But most impactful to me were the
haunting words that Chingachgook, the last living Mohican,
spoke at the end of the movie. He is standing on a high bluff,
looking out over the tree-blanketed wilderness that is his
home. And he speculates on what will become of the land. He
imagines the people who will come after him, what they will
be like, and what they will make of their lives in that place.
Then he says something with the slow force of a momentous
pronouncement: "But, once, *we were here.*" These words shook
me deeply.

Could we say something like this? At one level, this seems
to be a ridiculous question. I am Joe, and I am here. So, yes,
of course I can say that once I was here. But to what degree
am I here? To what degree have I shown up for my own life?
This is not a ridiculous question, but an existential and crucial
one. We are all "approximately" who God made us to be, but

not fully. For some of us, the approximation is good and we have—to a reasonable degree—shown up for our lives. For others of us, however, the approximation is not as good and we have work to do.

We are stewards of our lives. We must do the work required to cooperate with God's initiative to help us show up as the men we were created to be.

All my Christian life, Jesus stood at the door and knocked (Revelation 3:20). The consistent theme of His activity was that He wanted to be with me in the truth of myself, to co-inhabit places of my heart where I was still alone, living apart from Him (and even myself). This co-inhabitation is the slow, progressive filling of the Spirit. It is not the instantaneous filling that we so often pray for and so rarely experience. The slow and steady expansion of our home together with Jesus is genuine relationship that brings His presence, influence, truth, love, and healing to all areas of our hearts, including those we have repressed. These hidden parts of ourselves have deep historical and relational roots that make them impervious to superficial attempts to put them off. We must actively engage them *relationally* with Jesus.

Dr. John Coe said, "The degree to which we aren't aware of what is in our hidden heart is the degree to which it controls our experience of life."[13] I wholeheartedly agree. I would go still further and say this: to whatever degree we haven't dealt with our hidden hearts, we will feel more like "guys" than men. Or, we will embrace a concept of manhood that is malformed, conforming or reacting to our repressed material rather than reflecting God's design. We shall not be whole

---

13 From Dr. John Coe's course, "Introduction to Christian Spirituality," Talbot School of Theology, La Mirada, CA, October 2008.

men, but architects of our own images using materials that are only remains.

Crucial to transformation is our acceptance of a fundamental truth: whatever we suppress does not go away. It doesn't dissipate. It remains and sets itself up against our growth in the Spirit. Therefore, we must deal directly with this repressed content. We cannot ignore or minimize it. Nor can we simply try harder to counter it, pray it away through quick prayers of repentance and supplication, or overcome it through heightened accountability. We may try these approaches, but Ephesians 4:22 seems to require a more active "putting off."

We must take this action relationally—we can do nothing apart from Jesus (John 15:5). We abide in Him. We co-inhabit these areas of our heart with Him so that we are no longer alone in them. Together with Jesus, we come more and more under His love and influence. We take back parts of ourselves that we gave over to things that were not good for us. And we grow in love, freedom, substance, depth, power, authenticity. We come more alive as the men we were created to be.

And we don't need a two-year sabbatical or a three-week retreat to help us identify repressed material. Life will teach us where we need to focus!

When we think about honestly sharing more of our hearts with God and inviting Him into areas of sin, failure, guilt, shame, wounded-ness, immaturity, falseness, sadness, etc., we can feel directionless at first. How do we find these areas of our hearts that we need to invite God into? Or, if we see *many* places in our hearts where we are still alone, how do we know which of these places we should focus on?

These are important questions, and both have the same answer: life will teach us. God is constantly working in our lives—directly and indirectly—to show us the way. Directly, God may reveal to us particular areas of our hearts that need His attention. What is He currently showing you? Is there an area of your heart that regularly surfaces when you read Scripture, pray, listen to sermons, watch movies, read books? If there is, ask God if He wants you to engage with Him in this area and let Him love, guide, and transform you.

Indirectly, God may use our circumstances or other people to surface parts of our hearts that He wants us to open to Him and invite Him into. Maybe in your current circumstances, something leaks out of your heart more than usual. You might find yourself frequently impatient, for example, or routinely overcome with lust or anger. Others might also give you feedback about something they experience with you. They may be frustrated by your persistent insecurity and attempts to control them, for example. There could be any number of things leaking from your heart or being reflected back to you by others. If there is, this leakage or feedback may be an invitation from God.

I encourage you, therefore, to simply ask God, "What's the most important area I need to invite You into?" Then, let life show you the answer. There is no need to strain yourself looking for the answer, and there is no reason to be overwhelmed if there seem to be many possibilities. No need to rush either; it's okay to let the question "breathe" while you remain open to whatever answer takes shape.

Once you have identified an area of your heart to invite God into, simply begin by talking it over with Him. Maybe it's anger, for example: "Lord, I am so angry right now. Please be with me in my outrage—I don't want to be alone in this. What am I irritated about? Is it this thing that has happened right in front of me? Is it deeper? Where does my anger come from, Lord? How did it get there?" Once you start the conversation with God, be open to His leading and to any resources He might bring to help you in this area of your heart. Live with Him in this place over time. He will shepherd you. And be humble and courageous if He leads you to get help from others.

God is wise, and His insight is flawless. He knows what areas of our repressed hearts need His presence the most. It would be impossible in our lifetime to see and co-inhabit every part of our hidden hearts with God, but He knows where the centers of gravity are—those places that, if healed, would bring us the fullest experience of our masculine design. He will guide us.

LOOKING BACK AND LEANING FORWARD

God's guidance is much clearer to me now as I look back over my life with Him so far. He has been in everything. But what stands out to me is my Father's heart and His love. I see a God who relentlessly pursues me, using all things to draw me into an authentic relationship that truly transforms. This relationship is, therefore, both an end in itself and a means to an end: it leads to more healing and to flourishing as the man God created me to be.

However, I must clearly relay a fundamental truth: the journey never ends. I continue to discover places in my heart where I am broken and alone. In fact, these last eight years since my three-week retreat have been some of the most difficult for me. I've run into life circumstances—particularly in the last three years—that cracked open my heart and exposed some tough truths about myself. I was surprised by the depth of brokenness I encountered and my need for God's intensive healing. In one case, I needed more courage than I have ever had to muster before.

It's safe to say, then, that I am still on this journey with you! At the same time, I want to be careful not to minimize the growth I've experienced. I am radically changed, and I am changing. I feel freer, more at peace, and more substantial and joyful than ever. I've simply had to accept that discovery of broken places in my heart is a "new normal" for me and that it ultimately leads to fuller life. As I share these places as honestly as I can with God, He consistently—and persistently—uses whatever I uncover to expand His home with me and bring more growth to my masculine soul.

So, let us resolve together that we will do what men do: we will walk straight into the difficult things. We won't sacrifice fuller life and greater influence—for our families, churches, and communities—for the comfort of avoidance. We will muster the courage to be weak and find healing and wholeness in the One Who loves us.

And how far will we go? As I mentioned earlier, we are approximations of the men God created us to be. The Fall and all of its consequences have taken their toll. Therefore, I don't believe that we can become *comprehensively* the men God made us to be in this life. But we can sure become closer approximations! With this growth comes a great reward: more fullness of life in our masculine design. We change dramatically over time—we are not the men we were last year, and we are not the men we will be next year. This radical transformation is the promise of Romans 8:28-29 and John 10:10. Be encouraged, brothers—more growth and life are coming! It just takes time, because our growth is relational.

Finally, I leave you with this—one of my favorite stories that reflects the hope I have for myself and for you. During the Civil War, General Sherman and General Grant became deeply devoted friends. Sherman once wrote to Grant, "I knew wherever I was that you thought of me, and that if I got in a tight place you would come if alive."[14]

These words echo other occasions when Sherman spoke of Grant as a brother. But what strikes me most about the relationship between these two men is not their dependence upon one another in the crucial moments of a momentous war. What moves me is Sherman's depiction of his friend after Grant's death. I hope the same can be said of me and of you: "He was a man all over, rounded and complete."[15]

FOR PRAYER AND DISCUSSION

Consider these questions with God and, if possible, write down your reflections.

1. God, what is the most important area of my heart that I need to invite You into right now? If I listen to my life, what is my experience telling me?

2. Please co-inhabit this place in my heart with me, Lord. I want to explore this part of myself together with You and experience Your love and guidance. Help me begin an honest conversation with You that leads me over time to

---

14   Grant and Sherman: The Friendship That Won the Civil War, Charles B. Flood, Harper Perennial, 2006, page 401.

15   American Experience DVD: Ulysses S. Grant, Warrior President, 2005, closing scene.

more healing, freedom, and a fuller experience of robust masculinity.

3. Please read the appendix. What parts of the appendix do you find most helpful? What questions do you still have? Take some time to bring these questions to God and talk them over with Him.

NOTE: For those of you interested in receiving spiritual direction, I recommend the Evangelical Spiritual Directors Association (ESDA). ESDA is located at:

https://www.graftedlife.org/spiritual-direction/esda#

The website has a feature that enables you to search for an approved spiritual director who might be able to meet with you either in person or remotely via video or phone.

SAFE PASSAGE

THROUGHOUT THIS BOOK WE HAVE SEEN THAT it is logical and, most importantly, biblical, to open our hearts to God and invite Him into areas where we may still be alone. These areas include places of sin, failure, guilt, shame, wounded-ness, immaturity—all of it. However, some of us may still have reservations about this type of self-examination based on genuine concerns that also seem to carry scriptural weight. We need to address these concerns to establish the theological confidence required to freely enter into parts of our repressed hearts with God.

Over the years, I've talked with many evangelicals—pastors and congregants—who have had reservations about looking at our hearts with God. I have found their concerns to be sincere and very thoughtful, and I want to thoughtfully address them. In the following pages I attempt to do just that. There are eight concerns that I find most common, and so I will address them one by one.

1 GOD CANNOT LOOK UPON SIN

We know that God is holy; He is light and there is no darkness in Him (1 John 1:5). Many of us believe that, since God is holy, He cannot look upon sin, not even the sin in the hearts of His children. There is one verse in particular that seems to bear this out:

> You who are of purer eyes than to see evil and cannot look at wrong, why do you idly look at traitors and remain silent when the wicked swallows up the man more righteous than he?
>
> —Habakkuk 1:13

On the surface, this verse appears to be straightforward support for the conclusion that God cannot even look upon sin. However, the original language (Hebrew) contains a critical nuance that compels us to change our conclusion. And the rest of Scripture, in particular Jesus' ministry, shows that God can and does look at sin.

Habakkuk 1:13 is part of Habakkuk's complaint to God that wicked men seem to prosper and go unpunished. In Hebrew, both the word he uses for "see" and the word he uses for "look" have something in common—the element of favor or approval. Another way to look at the verse, then, would be something like this:

> You who are of purer eyes than to approvingly behold evil and cannot look with favor at wrong, why do you idly regard traitors and remain silent when the wicked swallows up the man more righteous than he?

Habakkuk's complaint is that God seems to be doing what His character will not allow Him to do: look upon sin with favor, approval, or regard. Habakkuk was incredulous that God was silent and did not punish those who were abusing His people. And he correlated silence and lack of action with favor or approval. God answers his complaint by assuring him that retribution will come at its appointed time.

In addition to this understanding of Habakkuk 1:13, we have Jesus' ministry to examine. How did He deal with sin while He was among us? He seemed to move straight towards it. Coming to live among us put Him right in the middle of everything; He must have seen sin all around Him every day. And He moved toward, not away from those caught in its power. He spent time with sinners (Matthew 9:11), and He told His disciples that the sick are the ones who need a physician (Matthew 9:12-13). He even took all our sins upon Himself; He *became* sin for us (2 Corinthians 5:21).

God is not threatened by sin; His holiness and integrity are never at risk in the presence of sin. Surprisingly, He allowed Satan—the father of sin—to speak to Him concerning Job (Job 2:1-8). He is altogether "other" and forever will be. However, it is important to remember that sin cannot remain unchanged in God's presence. Rather, sin is exposed in His presence (Isaiah 6:5) and eradicated (Hebrews 12:29).

2 JESUS SAID THAT NOTHING GOOD COMES FROM THE HEART

I met with a pastor for lunch not long ago who wondered why we would pay so much attention to our hearts if Jesus said that nothing good comes from them. His concern has merit. After all, if Jesus said that nothing good comes from the heart, shouldn't we disregard and bypass our hearts in the process of transformation and focus on cognitive and behavioral change? We could, and many of us do. However, this approach to growth severely stunts our development. Therefore, we need to address this pastor's concern, and the best way to ease his apprehension is to discuss it in two parts. First, we will determine whether or not Jesus actually said that nothing good comes from the heart. Then, we will address the underlying and critical question: does Jesus want to be with us in the places of our hearts that are "bad"?

First, I find no record of Jesus having said that nothing good comes from the heart. Nor do I see a statement like this in the rest of the New Testament. Rather, many people I have talked with refer to Jeremiah 17:9:

The heart is deceitful above all things and desperately sick; who can understand it?

Paul also picks up on the deceitful nature of our hearts in his letter to the Ephesians (emphasis mine):

...*to put off your old self, which belongs to your former manner of life and is corrupt through deceitful desires,* and to be renewed in the spirit of your minds, and to put on the new self, created after the likeness of God in true righteousness and holiness.

—Ephesians 4:22-24

These verses from Paul indicate that our hearts are not comprehensively bad, but a mixture of both good and bad. I'm sure we can agree that it would be inappropriate to say that nothing good comes from the hearts of regenerated believers who have faith in Jesus and the indwelling Holy Spirit. To whatever degree we have been able to put on the new self in Christ, there is goodness in our hearts.

The real question is, how do we put off the old self?[16] Does Jesus want us to bring the "bad" parts of our hearts into relationship with Him? It is very instructive to read through the Gospels and see how often Jesus makes insightful comments or asks penetrating questions to reveal the truth of what is in His hearers' hearts. The heart appears to be the center of action in His ministry, as He highlights in many places, including these verses, in Luke and Matthew:

> The good person out of the good treasure of his heart produces good, and the evil person out of his evil treasure produces evil, for out of the abundance of the heart his mouth speaks.
>
> —Luke 6:45

> But what comes out of the mouth proceeds from the heart, and this defiles a person.
>
> —Matthew 15:18

Since the heart is the center of action in the Christian life, we must put off whatever is in our hearts from our former manner of life (Ephesians 4:22). We cannot do this alone (John 15:5). We must be with Jesus. He is the Physician who can heal the sick parts of our hearts (Matthew 9:12-13). Therefore, let us be honest with God and, in dependence, invite Him to

---

16   See Section 5 of this Appendix for a discussion of the word "mind."

be with us and expand His home with us—especially in areas of our hearts that are "defiled." He is understanding, merciful, and gracious (Hebrews 4:15-16). He will love and help us; He will change us.

3 IF WE LOOK DEEPLY INTO OUR HEARTS, WE WILL GET OVERWHELMED OR LOST

The man who expressed this concern to me has been in fruitful ministry for over 40 years. As we talked, it became clear that he has seen glimpses of the darkness in his own heart and in the hearts of others. As he imagined the totality of what might be in our hearts, he felt it could be overwhelming and unsafe to enter. He is a shepherd, and he wants to steer his flock clear of danger.

I was quick to agree with him on one point: *if it were possible* to see and experience a significant portion of our repressed hearts, we could get overwhelmed or lost. Not only is there sin and vice deep in our hearts, but also whatever wounds we suffered and, typically, feelings of sadness, loneliness, anger, guilt, and shame. However, we are two steps removed from any danger. First, we can't see or experience too much of these deeply troubled places of our hearts; we have built-in defense mechanisms that prevent overexposure. And we don't *want* to see too much of these places; it is unnecessary.

First, even if we intend to explore our anger, for example, we will not for this reason see or experience all of it. According to Dr. Betsy Barber, there is a layer of numbness that separates us from our anger and its deeper sources. We are generally resistant to penetrating this layer of numbness and exploring the deeper regions of our hearts as we see in the figure below.[17]

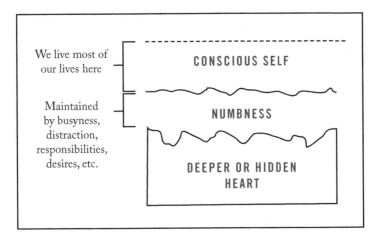

Therefore, our intentionality will enable us to see only so much. And if we ever do see or experience enough to make us feel extremely uncomfortable, we can always back away from it and ask somebody like a mentor, spiritual director, or Christian therapist to accompany us.

Also, we don't *want* to see too much of our deeper or hidden heart; we want to explore only what God wants us to explore. Fortunately, He does not ask us to see everything, only what is most necessary to remove the largest blockages and propel us forward as He expands His home within us. He decides what places in our hearts we need to explore with Him, as we discussed in Chapter 8. After all, we need to know what we are "putting off" in order to put it off (Ephesians 4:22). However, we cannot know all that is in our hearts and put off all of the "old man" in this life. Only in Heaven will we

17   From the course, "Intensive Journey Inward and Retreat," Dr. Betsy Barber, Talbot School of Theology, La Mirada, CA, February 2009.

be completely filled with the Spirit and God will finally be "all in all" (1 Corinthians 15:28).

4 WE CANNOT TRUST OUR FEELINGS

Many of us believe that it is dangerous to look at our own hearts because we cannot trust the feelings that reside there. This might be the most common concern I hear: feelings are untrustworthy. We easily form this conclusion from experience; we all know what it is like to want to do something that would be unhelpful for us or even devastating for ourselves and others. Therefore, shouldn't right thinking and right behavior be enough to guide us in the Christian life? Wouldn't this way of living be safer than giving space to our feelings?

Our distrust of feelings is well founded, but it doesn't demand that we dismiss them altogether. In fact, our emotions can serve us both as *guides* and *indicators*. With careful discernment, they can lead us into the will of God for us. And they can tell us when something is wrong and requires our attention.

FEELINGS AS GUIDES

Granted, allowing our emotions to lead us requires knowledge of the Scriptures and careful discernment, often with the help of others. After all, if we feel anxious, worried, afraid, angry, or lustful, for example, we do not want to automatically take action on these feelings. They could easily lead us into sin. Rather, our first move is to ask God to help us follow the Scriptures in these emotions:

EMOTION	FIRST MOVE
Anxious	Cast all of your anxieties on Jesus; remember, He cares for you (1 Peter 5:7).
Afraid	Do not worry; remember, God knows what you need (Matthew 6:32-34).
Worried	Remember, the Lord is your Helper; do not be afraid (Hebrews 13:6).
Angry	Do not sin in your anger; do not let anger linger past the day (Ephesians 4:26).
Lustful	Flee from lust (1 Corinthians 6:18).

If we make this first move to obey the Word and persevere in it, our feelings may change. If they do, this is wonderful! It means our character and emotions have followed the intention of our will to trust God and obey Him.

Of course, even if the emotions we experience are positive, we do not necessarily follow them. A man or woman may feel excited and happy about a decision to become involved with someone other than their spouse, for example. We know not to follow this excitement and happiness as indications of the "good way" when it would clearly be contrary to Scripture and horribly destructive.

However, we don't want to view our feelings as threatening. They can be revealing leaders. God made each of us uniquely, and He has woven within us desires that are congruent with His purposes for us. Deep within, our desires can point the way toward our destinies, as well as the "smaller" things we might do on any given day. The question, "What do you want to do?" is a critical question in our discernment. It could lead us to a particular vocation, a married or single life, children, loving acts for friends and family, various and effective ministries, creativity, beauty, hobbies that replenish us. The list goes on and on. And as we grow closer and closer to Jesus, our desires become more sanctified and trustworthy:

> Delight yourself in the Lord, and he will give you the desires of your heart.
>
> —Psalm 37:4

Therefore, three recommendations will keep us safe as we consider our emotions in decision-making:

1. Draw close to God.
2. Obey God in the Scriptures.
3. Include the wise counsel of mature believers.

FEELINGS AS INDICATORS

In addition to the potential to serve as leaders or guides, our feelings can also tell us when something is wrong. Refer again to the table of emotions in this section. What if we make the first move to obey the Word and persevere in this attempt, but our emotions persist, maybe chronically so? We continue to try to trust God and obey the Word, but it does not work for us; the emotions remain strong and unchanged. In this case, our feelings are telling us something is wrong; there is something in our character that opposes the intention of our will to trust God and obey Him. Our emotions, then, serve as an indicator of this opposition in our character, like a yellow or red light on the dashboard of our heart. It tells us that something is "off."

We can view the emotion, then, as an invitation from God. We can open it to Him and consider it with Him. We can ask, for example, "Lord, why is my fear so strong? What am I truly afraid of? Where does this fear come from? What is its source? What deep beliefs and desires does it hold?" This gives us the opportunity to invite God into this troubling feeling and whatever lies behind it so He can bring these realities into contact with His love and influence. We don't want to suppress the feeling or be alone in it and simply hope it will go away. Suppression always leaves our emotions untouched; they remain powerful and control much of our experience of life. We need Jesus with us in the truth of ourselves.

5 WE ARE TRANSFORMED ONLY THROUGH THE RENEWING OF OUR MINDS

This concern is also very common. It arises primarily from Romans 12:1-2 (emphasis mine):

> I appeal to you therefore, brothers, by the mercies of God, to present your bodies as a living sacrifice, holy and acceptable to God, which is your spiritual worship. Do not be conformed to this world, *but be transformed by the renewal of your mind,* that by testing you may discern what is the will of God, what is good and acceptable and perfect.

Concerned believers may say, "Why the need to look at our hearts if transformation comes by right thinking?" To address this important question, we need to ask two additional questions. First, what does the renewal of our minds actually mean? And second, what are we to do if we are not experiencing transformation in a particular area of life, despite thinking correctly about it?

When most of us think of renewing our minds, we tend to focus on our intellectual, cognitive, or rational faculties only.

However, as much as we evangelicals resist negative cultural influences, this understanding of the mind is a product of our culture. It is rooted in the Scientific Era begun in the 16th century. Paul had a more holistic view of the mind than we do in the modern era.

It is interesting to note where Romans 12:1-2 falls in Paul's letter to the Romans. In Chapter 11, he exhorts the Gentiles to humility and worship in light of God's wisdom and mercy in saving them. Because of God's wisdom and mercy, he says, we are to worship God by presenting ourselves as living sacrifices; we are not to conform to this world, but be transformed by the renewal of our minds. And our transformation will manifest itself in the way we value, serve, and genuinely love one another (Romans 12:3-21). This interpersonal fruit is the good and acceptable and perfect way Paul mentions in verse 2.

Therefore, whatever we do in renewing our minds, it is to produce Christlikeness in how we live. And this Christlikeness is more than behavioral change; it is behavioral change that flows freely from a changed heart. The mind and the heart are inextricably linked. The Greek definition of "mind" bears this out. The mind comprises our faculties to perceive and understand, as well as the faculties of feeling, judging, and determining.[18] In the context of Romans 12:2, in particular, Paul emphasizes our *reason* or our ability to perceive truth, understand what is good, and hate evil. Therefore, Paul seems to be saying that transformation begins but does not end with our understanding. Our understanding is to influence our faculties of feeling and judging as well (we hate evil, love genuinely, etc.). These are matters of the heart. If we are to be

---

18   The Greek definition of the mind is taken from Biblehub.com.

more like Jesus, we will exhibit the fruit of the Spirit *from the heart* (Galatians 5:22-23).

But what if we know the truth of God's Word in some area of life, but we are not able to obey freely from the heart? Intellectually we grasp the truth, but it does not translate to authentic behavioral change. As we discussed earlier, this is an indication that there is something in our character that opposes the intention of our will to obey the truth we see in God's Word. We want to open this area of our heart with God and ask Him to help us see what is going on. If we ignore it, override it in our own strength, or simply ask God to take it away, it likely will not change. God often deals with these places in our hearts in a more relational way; they are, in fact, doorways to a deeper experience of His presence with us and His love and transformation.

6 WE'RE SUPPOSED TO FORGET WHAT IS BEHIND; WE ARE NEW CREATIONS

This concern naturally emerges from Paul's statement in Philippians 3:13-14:

> Brothers, I do not consider that I have made it my own. But one thing I do: forgetting what lies behind and straining forward to what lies ahead, I press on toward the goal for the prize of the upward call of God in Christ Jesus.

Definitely, as Paul exhorts us in these verses, let us forget what is behind. However, let us be careful to forget what he actually tells us to forget. He tells us to forget the life of *confi-*

dence in the flesh,[19] confidence we put in our own human efforts to grow ourselves and attain righteousness before God.

Paul uses athletic imagery in his letter to the Philippians— he is intently focused on the race before him. The race represents our life of faith in Christ rather than human effort apart from God. This is why Paul starts chapter 3 with reference to the same Judaizers who infiltrated the Galatian church and persuaded some believers not to put their faith in Jesus only, but also to adhere to the Mosaic Law through circumcision (see Galatians 3). Paul attacks these Judaizers in Philippians 3, calling them "dogs" and "mutilators of the flesh." He then dismisses his own attempts at righteousness through human effort and calls all that he attained "rubbish." What matters to Paul is that he knows Christ and depends on Christ's righteousness freely given to him through faith. He resolves to live fully into the life of faith and all that God wants to do in him and through him.

We are to forget, then, our own efforts to make ourselves righteous—all efforts to fix ourselves and grow ourselves apart from God in our own strength. We are to give up on our own self-improvement project. As we discussed in Chapter 3, the Christian life is not "God's work, then our work." We do not try to measure up to God's standards or show our appreciation for Jesus' sacrifice for us by being the men He wants us to be and living the lives He desires for us *in our own power.*

Therefore, it cannot be Paul's intent to use Philippians 3:13 to suppress parts of our hearts that carry sin residue and other hidden material from our former lives. These are to be intentionally put off rather than repressed (see Ephesians

---

19   See his argument just prior to these verses, in the first half of Philippians 3.

4:22). What we are to leave behind is our dependence on our own efforts to grow ourselves and make ourselves righteous.

However, some believe Paul is making a more general statement in Philippians 3:13-14, telling us to forget more than just the life of self-effort, but all of the sin that came with it. We find a similar exhortation in Hebrews 12:1:

> Therefore, since we are surrounded by so great a cloud of witnesses, let us also lay aside every weight, and sin which clings so closely, and let us run with endurance the race that is set before us.

To this interpretation of Philippians 3:13-14, we also say, "By all means!" We should forget or let go of the encumbrances and sin that hold us back in the life of faith. However, if we try to let go of any particular sin, but it won't let go of us, we have work to do with Jesus. Again, we need to invite Him into this area of our heart with us and receive His truth, forgiveness, acceptance, love, and companionship.

7 LOOKING AT OUR OWN HEARTS IS A DISTRACTION FROM THE GREAT COMMISSION

Many people I've talked with worry that, if we look at our hearts, we will get lost in a kind of narcissistic self-exploration and forget about the Great Commission. They are deeply concerned for the millions of unreached people who may perish without Jesus. I admire their hearts for the lost. However, if we look at our own hearts as described in this book, we will not be distracted from the Great Commission in the short term. And, in the long term, it will enable a much more robust fulfillment of the Great Commission.

In the short term, God might show us some things in our hearts that require time and energy to address with Him. However, the imperatives in Scripture still stand. We are still called to love our neighbor (Mark 12:31), make disciples (Matthew 28:18-20), and remember the poor (Galatians 2:10). Can we allow God to show us whatever He wants us to see in our hearts and obey the commands in these verses at the same time?

If God is leading us to look honestly at ourselves, as well as care for others, we can do both. In fact, as we look at our own hearts, we grow in humility and develop our capacity to understand others and show compassion. I went through a long season in which God regularly showed me places in my heart that I needed to invite Him into. It was difficult at times. It was during this season, though, that God also led me to minister among the homeless near the Port of Los Angeles, as I mentioned earlier. I worked with a small team that met in a park for breakfast and Bible study with homeless men and women every Saturday morning. I served at the park for 11 years, and as my honesty with God grew, my compassion for these men and women grew. I learned more about ministry in those years than during any other time in my life.

Also, God used my interactions with the homeless to reveal more places of my heart that needed His presence, forgiveness, acceptance, love, and companionship. While I was trying to be obedient to God's call to serve the homeless, He also encouraged me to honestly share my experience of ministry with Him. There were many places in my heart of judgment, pride, selfishness, and anger that He revealed in those years of ministry. Together with Him in these places of my heart, sin began to soften and yield to deeper respect, love, and courage. The others on our team had similar experiences of God exposing sin and coming into these areas of vice in their hearts to transform them.

In the long term, opening our hearts to God enables the deepest possible fulfillment of the Great Commission. The more He transforms us, the more our character looks like Jesus' character. Jesus is "others-focused" and self-giving in all He does, so we will also become more others-focused and self-giving in all we do. This change will enable us to fulfill the Great Commission more freely and powerfully from the heart. Also, our motives will be purer in other ways: we will be more motivated out of concern for others and the glory of God rather than secret desires to maintain our idealized image of ourselves and keep feelings of failure, guilt, and shame at bay.

This growth in Christlikeness not only enables us to show deeper compassion for others, but become guides for them as well. Since we have looked (and continue to look) at our own hearts with Jesus, we become more relevant to the struggles with sin that others are facing. If we are more concerned about outward actions than the hearts from which these actions flow, we will be superficial Christians who are ill-equipped when faced with the interior struggles of others in disciple-making. Christians, above all, should be relevant to the real difficulties of others and be able to guide them in the way forward with Jesus.

8 OPENING AND LOOKING AT THE HEART SOUNDS LIKE PSYCHOLOGY

Many well-meaning Christians believe that the Word and faith are all we need for any emotional or psychological problem we face. In fact, some have come to see psychology as antithetical to Scripture and faith. I will take some time now to address this belief, then highlight my rationale for including several psychological principles in this book. Because, although God's Word and belief reign supreme, there are many other disciplines of study that inform our understanding of the Scriptures and support our life of faith.

Truth is truth wherever we find it. There was a time in Christian history when the leading scholars in the various sciences were all Christians. In medicine (study of the human body), anthropology (study of human cultures), sociology (study of human society), psychology (study of the human psyche), physics (study of the physical world), Christians sought to understand God's creation and how it works. All of these studies supported and informed their understanding of theology and the Scriptures[20]

Psychology, being one of these studies, attempts to address questions that are important to our life and well-being:

1. How has God designed the human psyche? How does it work?
2. What does healthy development of a person look like?
3. What kinds of things can go wrong?
4. What can we do to remedy maladies?

Truthful answers to these questions inform our understanding of the human condition and the Scriptures. Among other things, we come to better understand the devastating effects of original sin and our deep need for God. We also better understand why we believe some things about God in our gut that do not line up with our cognitive understanding of Scripture. For example, we assent to the biblical truth that God is involved in all of the details of our lives (Luke

---

20   During this time in Christian history (the Middle Ages), theology was called "The Queen of the Sciences." All the other sciences were "maid servants" of the queen.

12:22-31), yet we might struggle in our gut with the deep belief that He is somewhat distant from us and indifferent to the details of life that most concern us. Theologians refer to this difference between what we intellectually know—and assent to—and what we believe "in our gut" about God as the difference between our "God Concept" and "God Image," respectively.[21] We tend to project onto God the qualities of the early authority figures in our lives rather than deeply believe that God is who He says He is in the Scriptures.

I have included in this book only some basic psychological principles that help us better understand the Scriptures, like the principle described above (God Concept and God Image—see Mark 9:24). Another important principle included in this book is the principle of repression. Psychologists have known for generations that repressing feelings does not make them go away; they remain with us and can even grow stronger and control much of our experience of life. As a result, other mental and physical maladies may emerge. In my life, for example, I suffered from depression and high blood pressure because I repressed my feelings of anger.

The psychological principle that we should not repress our feelings, but work through them, lines up with scriptural imperatives to share everything with God and be with Him in reality (Psalm 62:8; Psalm 139:23-24, etc.). This principle also informs our understanding of commands in Scripture that tell us how to deal with the sin residue of our former manner of life, like Ephesians 4:22. We conclude in this verse, then, that "putting off the old man" does not mean "repressing the old man." Paul prescribes something more in this verse, some-

---

21   From the course, "Personality Development and Psychopathology," Dr. Betsy Barber, Talbot School of Theology, La Mirada, CA, February 2009.

thing less superficial and much more effective and lasting. If we are to put off the old man in the Spirit, it cannot look like repression.

It is also important to say a word about Christian therapy. The opportunity I've had to spend time in therapy has dramatically changed my life with God. He used my experience with several therapists to open my heart to Him in ways that were unimaginable to me. With their help, I was able to see so many places of my heart that were repressed and alone, separated from the presence and love of God. Even in the structure of my personality, I had built-in protective measures that kept distance between myself and God (and others as well).

With this said, I recommend we meet only with devout Christian therapists who conduct their work in context of a growing relationship with God and obedience to God in the Scriptures.

CLOSING

I hope these answers to common concerns have been helpful for you. It's important that you feel scripturally "safe" in entering deep places of your heart with God and inviting Him to co-inhabit these areas with you. May God grant you His peace as you journey on together in truth and love.

ACKNOWLEDGMENTS

WE WERE NOT MADE TO "GO IT ALONE" IN THIS life, and book-writing is no exception. I found that I needed others throughout the creative process to assist me and encourage me. And people showed up!

Thank you, Bryan Johnson, Karen Boden, and Drew Tilton for reviewing the manuscript and offering substantial and vitally important feedback. Karen, thanks also for taking the time to help make me a better writer. And, Bryan, I appreciate the times you helped propel me forward in this project when I got bogged down.

Thank you, Dr. John Coe, Dr. Betsy Barber, and Dr. Judy TenElshof for the direction and care you brought to my life in seminary and beyond. I wouldn't be writing if not for you.

Thank you, my friends and family, for the way you encouraged me throughout the writing process, a process that turned out to be a lot longer and harder than I imagined.

And thank you, publishing team—Drew Tilton, Jessica Snell, and Natalie Johnson—for your exceptional work on this book and your uplifting spirits.

Made in the USA
Las Vegas, NV
03 September 2021

29517061R00098